Practitioner's Toolbox Series

Building a Group Practice

Creating a Shared Vision for Success

American Psychological Association Practice Directorate
with
Coopers & Lybrand, L.L.P.

AMERICAN PSYCHOLOGICAL ASSOCIATION
Washington, DC

A Cautionary Note:

This manual was written to serve both as a reference and as a tool to help providers practice more efficiently in a changing, demanding marketplace. The information contained herein is accurate and complete to the best of our knowledge. However, *Building a Group Practice: Creating a Shared Vision for Success* should be read with the understanding that it is meant as a supplement, not a substitute, for sound legal, accounting, business, or other professional consulting services. When such services are required, the assistance of a competent professional should be sought.

Published by
American Psychological Association
750 First Street, NE
Washington, DC 20002

Copies may be ordered from
APA Order Department
P.O. Box 2710
Hyattsville, MD 20784

Composition and Printing: National Academy Press, Washington, DC
Cover Designer: Leigh Coriale

Library of Congress Cataloging-in-Publication Data
Building a group practice : creating a shared vision for success /
    American Psychological Association Practice Directorate with Coopers
    & Lybrand, L.L.P.
        p.   cm. — (Practitioners toolbox series)
        Includes bibliographical references.
        ISBN 1-55798-318-6 (alk. paper)
        1. Group practice in clinical psychology. 2. Group practice in
    clinical psychology—United States. I. American Psychological
    Association. Practice Directorate. II. Coopers & Lybrand.
    III. Series
    RC467.95.B85   1995
    616.89′0068—dc20   95-23749
                                                                                                        CIP

British Library Cataloguing-In-Publication Data
A CIP record is available from the British Library

Printed in the United States of America
First Edition

Contents

AMERICAN
PSYCHOLOGICAL
ASSOCIATION

Dear Colleague:

The American Psychological Association Practice Directorate is pleased to offer Building a Group Practice: Creating a Shared Vision for Success as one component of its "Practitioner's Toolbox" series written in conjunction with Coopers & Lybrand, L.L.P. This series of books is designed to help the practicing psychologist build a successful practice in an environment which requires attention to an increasingly complex approach to healthcare while maintaining the quality of services for which psychology has become known.

One particular trend ongoing in the healthcare system that has been reforming for years, is the integration and consolidation of service delivery. Previously separate and fragmented services, for example, are being pulled together in an effort to increase efficiency and decrease administrative costs. As a result, providers of healthcare are more and more joining together in groups to have access to segments of the marketplace for which group practice has advantages over the provision of services by solo practitioners. Multiple service groups and multidisciplinary groups are proving to be quite competitive where third party payers are looking to purchase a range of services through a single contract.

The inherent diversity of psychology is - or at least ought to be - a significant asset for us in an environment which values the ability to provide a variety of services. A psychology group practice, for example, able to provide pediatric, child, adolescent, adult, marriage and family, neuropsychology, rehabilitation, health psychology, and forensic services begins to maximize our profession's strength in the current healthcare climate. Even more so, a multidisciplinary group comprised of psychologists and primary care physicians approaches the type of "one stop shopping" valued by today's purchasers of healthcare.

Considerable, if not overwhelming, changes have occurred in the way healthcare services are delivered. Psychology's efforts to keep pace with these changes are necessary to insure our ability to fully participate in the new environment. Even more importantly, these efforts are critical to achieving a position for psychology in the healthcare marketplace with sufficient leverage to determine when psychological care is provided, how psychological services are provided, and who is appropriate to provide such services. It is only then that we can assure that consumers of psychological care are well-served.

Sincerely,

Russ Newman

Russ Newman, Ph.D., J.D.
Executive Director for Professional Practice

750 First Street, NE
Washington, DC 20002-4242
(202) 336-5913
(202) 336-5797 Fax
(202) 336-6123 TDD

Russ Newman, Ph.D., J.D.
Executive Director
Practice Directorate

Preface

Many psychologists enjoy the autonomy of owning their own practice. Self-owned practices offer the ultimate control and often make for rewarding careers. In this environment, clinicians have the greatest control over the style of behavioral health care they practice and their workplace environment. Practitioners often do not plan for their successes—they must account for the challenges of growth within the practice and changes in the market. Group practices offer practitioners the control, economies of scale, enhanced marketing, and other attributes to effectively compete in a continually evolving health care market.

A common scenario of an *unplanned* group practice may begin something like this: A successful practitioner enjoys a lucrative solo practice. Dr. John Doe works ardently to build a major clientele and surrounds himself with a small office that meets the patients' needs. He enjoys a growing reputation in his market and the life of autonomy. As his business grows, the pace becomes more hectic, and he responds to the increased demand by hiring an associate. This soon leads to a second associate. Issues that were not clearly evident as a solo practitioner now require urgent attention as the practice begins to move forward. Internally, decision making becomes more complex. Issues of treatment quality, finance, and administration are made ad hoc as the growing practice begins to take on a life of its own. The practitioner finds himself spending more time involved in the administration of the business than the actual practice of behavioral health care.

Practitioners often do not plan for their successes.

Our objective in this book is to help ensure that *you* plan for a successful group practice, whether your group practice results from an evolutionary process or is a conscious decision to transform a solo practice into a group practice to capitalize on changes in the market. Unplanned growth can lead to actions taken in haste. Although the ability to react to market conditions remains critical, planning allows the practitioner to control his or her own destiny, not simply respond to events. But what should the practice plan for? This text offers an opportunity to create shared visions for the group practice—to see the new practice not in today's successes but tomorrow's, not in infancy but maturity.

Let's first understand what the term "group practice" means.

> *A group practice is the organization of a group of practitioners as a private partnership, limited liability company, or corporation; participating practitioners share facilities and personnel as well as earnings from their practice. The providers comprising the practice may represent either a single specialty or a range of behavioral health specialties.*

Note that the above definition requires a *sharing* of revenues, costs, and ideas as well as the risks of the practice. A solo practitioner who contracts with multiple associates to handle excess capacity is not, by definition, a group practice since there is neither a shared vision nor a sharing of the financial and liability responsibilities of the practice.

The current reforms occurring in the delivery of mental health care present group practitioners with unique opportunities. This book is designed to assist you in considering new clinical practice and business dynamics of group practices. In this way, you will think through and plan for contingencies that result in sound decision making—not spur-of-the-moment reactions. Providers want control—control of their livelihood, practice philosophy, income, and source of patients. This text presents a blueprint for considering your own practice success.

Ultimately, successful practices must achieve clinical quality and business efficiencies.

PURPOSE OF THIS GUIDEBOOK

This book is one component of a "toolbox" commissioned by the American Psychological Association's (APA's) Practice Directorate to assist its membership in improving their practice dynamics—marketing, financial management, managed care contracting, selecting information systems, and other pertinent topics affecting behavioral health care providers.

Each book in the Practitioner's Toolbox Series has been written from a "how to" perspective. Every effort was made to focus on practical advice and guidance instead of theory or philosophy. For additional information, an extensive bibliography is included in each volume.

HOW TO USE THIS GUIDEBOOK

This guidebook is intended to shed light on critical issues affecting a group practice formation. It is not intended to be an alternative to competent legal and consulting advice to assist you in development and implementation; however, it offers a comprehensive guide to structure your thinking about the subject.

Group formation is a complex subject that requires abstract thinking. By this, we mean that steps in group formation do not necessarily lend themselves to "checklist" style, as they are not always sequential in nature. It will be difficult to "divide and conquer" sections of this book as decisions in one area are highly contingent on decisions made in other areas. For example, after the group decides on compensation of its members, as discussed in chapter 3, it must develop a legal structure and financial projections that support this decision. Therefore, it is recommended that this book be read in its entirety to permit a comprehensive understanding of the task at hand.

Later, as groups work through specific issues, the text may serve as a ready reference. A list of questions is included in chapter 8 to assist in identification of critical issues. These questions are arranged by major category for easier reference. Additionally, each chapter begins with an abstract outlining the key topics to be covered in the chapter.

Chapter 1 begins with an overview of the changing mental and behavioral health marketplace. The delivery and payment for mental health and behavioral health services continue to be redefined. Consolidations among payers, providers, insurers, and employers are occurring in rapid progression. This chapter introduces the reader to these market changes in reimbursement and service delivery and offers further motivation for the development of successful group practices in the future market. Nearly one out of every two insured Americans receives mental health care through managed care organizations or other systems of care. Therefore, discussion of market changes must include a general understanding of managed care's unique characteristics and incentives within the broader context of fundamental market reform.

Chapters 2 through 7 explore relevant topics of organizations and business planning, operations, financial management, governance, and legal structure. In chapter 2, we begin discussion of building a group practice by addressing development of a shared vision among the members. This will be the foundation upon which all later planning must be based. Additionally, chapter 2 introduces business planning and suggests a format to begin organizing and documenting the group's clinical and financial plan for success. The business plan is introduced early in the book to allow practitioners to understand the level of detail required to develop a more comprehensive document. Later, other chapters can help the reader focus on relevant issues and the business plan can be readdressed in earnest.

Chapter 3 discusses the dynamics that bring groups together and, unfortunately, can also lead to their demise. A discussion of group formation is hardly complete without first understanding what motivates practitioners to participate in group practices. This chapter dovetails with and is an extension of chapter 2's discussion of development of a group's vision. However, in this chapter, we look at needs from more of a group perspective rather than the individual's. At the end of the chapter, practitioners will have a greater understanding of group motivations, sources of power and conflict, and strategies for conflict resolution. As with chapter 2, our discussion seeks to further strengthen the foundation of a group practice before we build it.

Chapter 4, Operations, introduces the necessary practice and business considerations for clinical and financial success. The discussion also includes consideration of management information systems, marketing, and a discussion of clinical operations. In chapter 5, we discuss both issues of financing of the practice and relevant issues in financial management. The first part of the chapter explores various options in obtaining capital while the latter half is devoted more to a detailed discussion of determining costs for group services and a discussion of reimbursement. These topics are further discussed in the Toolbox book on financing your practice.

Governance is the process of determining how decisions will be made and how the practice will be managed. These issues are dealt with in chapter 6, which includes strategies for an effective board of directors. Chapter 7 helps the new group explore various options for a legal entity. The group must first decide issues of governance, compensation, shared goals, etc. before a proper legal structure can be selected that supports the new practice's vision. The text looks at each structure's tax and governance advantages and disadvantages. Antitrust concerns are also addressed.

Finally, chapter 8 is a comprehensive list of questions designed to help your group answer critical questions to key issues. You may wish to add to this list as you work through the planning process.

...group success hinges on balancing the development of both functional group dynamics and effective practice management and planning.

This book attempts to strike a balance between the abstract group formation issues and the more concrete business planning issues. Group formation is not an easy task, but at stake is the control of each member's livelihood. It is clear that group success hinges on balancing the development of both functional group dynamics and effective practice management and planning. Individuals who come together with an understanding of each other's practice philosophy and management style, but no appreciation for financial planning, are doomed to failure. Similarly, a comprehensive business plan with detailed financial projections and operational timelines is inadequate if group formation issues are ignored. Successful practice development is not simply the flawless execution of a good business plan (although it certainly helps!)—it is a complex blending of cultures, clinical and managerial philosophies, and shared goals. As you read this book, try to find the right balance among all issues, draw on individual strengths, and plan for the unexpected.

Acknowledgments

We are grateful for the contributions of the following people whose hard work and assistance made this book possible: the Coopers and Lybrand staff, headed by Ron Bachman, FSA, MAAA, and Ron Finch, EdD, and including Wanda Bishop, Phil Kalafut, Tina Kind, Al Schellhorn, Don Weber, and Monte Weisenberger; Russ Newman, PhD, JD, Henry Engleka, and Jeffrey Zimmerman, PhD, as well as the APA Practice Directorate Marketing Department staff, including Neela Agarwalla, JD, Garth Huston, Craig Olswang, and Chris Vein.

1

The Changing Mental and Behavioral Health Market

ALTHOUGH COMPREHENSIVE, *national health reform died in the halls of Congress in 1994, market reform continues to occur. The health care industry is characterized by rapid change in the delivery and reimbursement of care. This is in part driven by the increased sophistication in purchasing strategies of payers and insurers who demand more efficient and appropriate delivery of behavioral health care services. To develop an effective business strategy that increases provider control of the clinical and economic aspects of the practice, practitioners need to have a clear understanding of the changing marketplace.*

This chapter has a twofold mission: first, to introduce group practices as a successful strategy to compete in markets where delivery of behavioral health care is driven by systems of care, and second, to describe market dynamics as they drive this redesign of health care.

WHY FORM A GROUP PRACTICE?

Group practices continue to form as an effective strategy for meeting the evolving demands of an increasingly sophisticated market. What is the fundamental change driving this need? Undoubtedly, it is the changed relationship among providers, patients, and third party payers or insurers. Before the most recent market reform, companies assumed a benefit structure that provided payment based on treatment decisions decided entirely by the patient and provider, essentially a fee for service market. Faced with escalating health care costs and associated loss of competitiveness, employers and other payers sought means to influence the purchasing decision of health care and, thus, be a part of the link in service delivery between patient and provider. Payers of health care also sought to simplify administration by contracting for multiple services all at one time. Insurers, with expertise in timely payment of claims, also failed to understand employers' needs for *systems* of care that provide savings and management of the delivery system.

Group practices form as an effective means of integrating systems of behavioral health care. The following reflects an overview of reasons to consider group practices and why group practices allow for better transition into systems of care:

- ✔ *Economies of Scale.* Group practices typically consolidate the administrative and management functions of solo practitioners and therefore lower administrative overhead. This sharing of resources ultimately lowers the practice's costs and increases competitiveness. Though potentially one of the greatest advantages of group affiliation, groups sometimes do not enjoy economies when they fail to consolidate staffs and other resources.

- ✔ *Enhanced Negotiating Position.* Systems of care, today and in the future, look to lower *their* administrative costs by signing multiple providers (and/or specialties) with one single contract. When a practice eases the administrative burden on a system of care, the group increases its own competitiveness.

- ✔ *Greater Market Access.* Group providers may have greater geographic access to patients than solo practitioners.

- ✔ *Pooled Capital.* Group practices can pool the capital resources of each practitioner to defray costs that may be prohibitive to the solo practitioner, such as management information systems, office space, start-up funding, etc.

- ✔ *Sharing of Risk.* Group practices have greater flexibility to share the clinical and financial risks of operating under risk-sharing contracts and also the business risk associated with owning and operating the practice. Legal entities can be formed that minimize personal liability (discussed further in chapter 7).

- ✔ *Enhanced Peer Consultation.* Group practices offer the opportunity to share clinical experience with other practitioners.

- ✔ *Control.* Group practices (particularly multispecialty groups) have greater control over their referral source. Groups that offer multiple specialties in multiple locations offer the "one stop shopping" desired by systems of care and therefore are in enhanced negotiating positions.

✔ *Strategic Advantages.* The current health care market is characterized by the development of systems of care known as "integrated delivery systems," that is, systems that integrate the services of practitioners, hospitals, clinics, residential treatment centers, and other facilities along a defined continuum of care. Group practices are in an excellent position to either contract with, develop, or in some cases, own equity stakes in these systems of care. Integrated delivery systems are further discussed in this chapter.

What market forces drive this need for systems of care? Essentially, the health care market is undergoing a radical redesign in both the delivery and the reimbursement of services. This is characterized by a decrease in fee for service contracting and a requirement that providers generate reports verifying appropriate and efficient use of the health care premium. This chapter further explains the market forces that make group practices a viable competitive choice for practitioners.

Private Pay or Third Party Reimbursement?

Participation as a group practitioner is a most effective strategy for competing for third party reimbursement. Some group practices depend solely on third party reimbursement, while others develop a comfortable niche market among private paying patients or patients that choose to exercise their benefits outside of the benefit plan's selected providers. Some choose to mix their business while others prefer to keep third party reimbursement a very small part of the group's clientele—just enough to understand the differing style of behavioral health care required to practice in a system of care. The decision whether or not to mix business among private pay or third party reimbursement is contingent on the group practitioners' financial goals, size of the local private payer market, and an understanding of the style of behavioral health care practitioners wish to pursue.

Many groups find niche markets outside of third party reimbursement. Perhaps the group delivers a certain specialty or quality of service that commands a premium or a high percentage of private payers. Clearly, this is market dependent. Should the group wish to pursue this option, a careful analysis of potential market share is critical. The private payer segment, in most markets nationwide, is decreasing. By the end of 1993, nearly 40% of the total population received its medical benefits through a health maintenance organization (HMO) or preferred provider organization (PPO) plan. By year-end 1994, that figure was closer to 50%. This trend puts pressure on practitioners to achieve proportionally greater market share for a dwindling number of private pay patients. Simply stated, practitioners are competing for a smaller private pay market. This strategy can be quite effective and rewarding under the right market conditions and with the right product for your particular market.

The remainder of this chapter explores the market changes that affect the delivery and reimbursement of mental health services and development of systems of care.

MARKET REFORM

The 1980s and the early 1990s were characterized by unprecedented growth in the delivery of psychiatric and chemical dependency care. The number of private free standing psychiatric and chemical dependency hospitals more than doubled, while the number of medical/surgical hospitals offering psychiatric or chemical dependency care increased more than 25%.

Corresponding to this growth, employers, insurance companies, and other payers saw their year-to-year costs for mental health care increase at a rate that more than doubled the Medical Consumer Price Index. Companies reported that mental health costs had grown to 15 to 25% of their total costs for health care, with some reporting costs beyond 25%. In response to these cost pressures, many employers and insurance companies began implementing managed care initiatives. In many markets, managed mental health care is aggressively pursued.

Managed care is a means of providing health care services within a defined network of health care providers who are given the responsibility to manage and provide quality, cost-effective care. These providers have procedures in place to ensure that only medically necessary and appropriate use of health care services occurs. Historically, admissions to psychiatric and chemical dependency care have been defined by the provider of record, who determined the intensity and length of care. The advent of managed care changed this by implementing protocols that define admission criteria and period of confinement.

In times past, the economics of patient care was characterized by the psychologist and patient agreeing on a course of treatment, with payment being the responsibility of employers and insurance companies. Ultimately, uncontrolled increases in health care costs stimulated the implementation of managed care which changed the treatment decision process by inserting the payer, or the payer's managed care agent, as a third party. Payers have, therefore, demanded reduced costs, shorter lengths of stay, and new modes of care.

As the market continues its reform, providers are increasingly required to deliver services along the mental health "continuum of care," generally defined as residential treatment, inpatient, partial hospitalization, home health, and outpatient services. Payers are increasingly requiring that psychologists not only practice along this continuum, but also provide measurable outcomes.

In general, the market has explored various methods to control health care costs. Approaches that have been used extensively include cost controls (e.g., negotiated reduced rates, capitation payments, fee schedules, per diem payments, and prospectively set prices based on diagnoses) and

---

As the market continues its reform, providers are increasingly required to deliver services along the mental health "continuum of care."

---

utilization controls (e.g., precertification, second opinion, utilization review requirements, case management, and discharge planning). Cost controls tend to be financial agreements that do not involve the payer in treatment decisions made by providers. Utilization controls may influence treatment decisions since they monitor care, attempting to ensure that only appropriate and medically necessary care is being provided. Utilization controls also strive to ensure that care is provided by the appropriate provider in the least costly, most appropriate setting.

This continual evolution on the part of the health care community to contain and, in fact, lower costs has met with mixed results. Within the last decade, payers of care have opted to place providers "at risk" for the delivery of their services; namely, each provider or system of care is prepaid for all services and required to provide care within a fixed budget. Group practices today are in a transition period when they must begin to shape their clinical practice of behavioral health care to compete in this new dynamic. In general, group practices will be rewarded, in terms of higher fixed prepayments, for their ability to accept the financial risk of providing services.

Changing Payment Structures

One of the single largest dynamics in the changing health care market is the assumption of financial risk by the providers of care. Managed care has ushered in an era where the lines between insurer and provider are not well delineated since both assume financial risk under certain conditions. Assumption of risk for services occurs at all levels in the delivery system, although its form varies from market to market. Fundamentally, across the nation, providers are being put "at-risk" for their services with a shift in incentives for the practitioner from operating in a fee for service environment to a capitated environment. These two terms and their financial incentives are defined below:

- *Fee for Service.* In the traditional fee for service model, the provider bills the consumer or payer for a specified amount, typically on the basis of the amount of time spent delivering the service. Until recently, the provider determined the fee charged for the service and customary fees were generally accepted. Now, the provider may be required to accept a payer's fee schedule, which demands a certain fee be accepted as payment in full. PPOs represent an attempt to save the fee for service method of payment by regulating the cost of treatment in the context of a traditional reimbursement plan.
- *Capitation.* In a capitated system, a provider or group of providers agrees (within defined parameters) to deliver all of the mental health care services required by a given population for a fixed cost per member. In this system, providers assume financial risk for a given population because payment to the provider is the same regardless of the amount or cost of care rendered.

Consider these statistics that mirror the changes in the mental health community: Three out of four office-based physicians in private practice participated in at least one managed care plan in 1994—up from 67% in 1992. Together HMO and PPO reimbursement represented 38% of a typical doctor's gross income compared with 22% in 1993. During that period, the size of the total market remained essentially unchanged. Thus, proportionally, private pay patients represented a smaller percentage of market total revenue available. This does not necessarily imply that third party contracting is the answer for your practice. It does, however indicate a major shift in reimbursement that groups must consider. Give local market dynamics serious consideration in your planning. Determine the market share required to meet the group's practice goals. If the required market share for private pay patients is too high to attain in your market, how will the group mix in third party business? If the group is multispecialty, will all services be offered in third party contracting?

Changing Financial Incentives: Risk Versus Reward

Payers and providers can work together to develop successful relationships in which they share the risks and rewards of providing health care coverage. Risk sharing provides a direct incentive for each party to take responsibility for ensuring that only cost-sensitive, high quality care is provided. To be successful, practitioners draw an appropriate balance between desired risk and reward. Those parties that share the risk will also share the rewards of ensuring that services are delivered in a sound and appropriate manner that is sensitive to costs. This implies that groups considering third party reimbursement options strive to push internal costs as low as possible to permit favorable, risk-sharing contracts.

In the past, insurers accepted premiums and financial risk for the provision of health care services in return for a set premium. Today, lines between insurers and providers of health care are no longer so easily discerned. Managed care organizations that accept risk contracting are coming under increased regulation by state insurance agencies. As they accept financial risks, states are requiring stricter compliance with laws governing licensure and capital requirements once only required of insurance entities. The concept is simple: If you act like an insurer, you will be regulated like an insurer.

Insurers, too, are becoming indistinguishable from providers. Big insurance plans compete head-to-head with managed care organizations and often market and promote their programs' "health care plans." For the group practice, contracting with a managed care organization and an insurer may be indistinguishable. This trend, though, is further evidence of the consolidation of the health care market among providers and insurers, often under prepaid capitated contracts.

How Does Capitation Work?

Under capitated arrangements, practitioners contract for a certain array of services for which they are 100% financially and clinically accountable. Financially, this means that if a group performs the services within the allotted fixed budget, it keeps the surplus and, conversely, it absorbs the losses for excessive services. Actuarial modeling can assist your practice in determining the scope of services to offer and your potential financial risk (referred to as your "exposure"). Clinical responsibility means that practitioners are responsible for the successful treatment outcomes of their patient through all levels of the continuum of care and for the entire duration of the illness. The provider continues to provide behavioral health care at the negotiated fixed price for all services in all modalities. The provider receives no additional payments beyond the per member per month fee. For this reason, capitated pricing is quite complex and should be conducted with an experienced actuary. This topic is also discussed in the Toolbox book covering the subject of contracting on a capitated basis. Practitioners must be aware of the scope of services for which they assume liability in their managed care contracts and ensure that the practice can perform these services in a high quality manner that manages the costs of delivery. This concept is further discussed in chapter 5.

DEVELOPMENT OF NEW DELIVERY SYSTEMS

Throughout the mental health and behavioral market, providers are organizing themselves to effectively deliver behavioral health care within systems of care. The result of this reorganization, and rethinking, about health care services is the emergence of the integrated delivery system (IDS). These systems offer "one stop shopping" to potential payers, meaning, that a payer can write "one check" for the entire delivery of mental and behavioral health care for its employees without having to negotiate terms with multiple, unconnected providers. IDSs offer a full continuum of care so that the patient (and premiums) are managed within one accountable plan's network of providers. IDSs coordinate the continuity of care, provide easy access, quantify and standardize quality, reduce clinical and administrative redundancy, align provider incentives (practitioner and hospital), and provide for easier contracting and marketing to third party payers.

Integrated delivery systems are extremely competitive in their pricing, often 15% to 25% below their competitors. The term "integrated," as it applies to health systems, implies the following:

- *Breadth of Integration*—IDSs serve multiple diagnoses along a continuum of behavioral health care.
- *Depth of Integration*—Refers to the number of providers offering the same kinds of services.
- *Horizontal Integration*—Horizontally integrated providers offer the same services over a defined geographic area. In this way, patients are guaranteed access to services regardless of their location in the region. Horizontally integrated programs also ensure that programs offer the same credentials and standards for quality. Group practices help integrated systems achieve this goal by consolidating providers in one or more locations.
- *Vertical Integration*—Indicates the degree of linkages among practitioners, suppliers, and the parent health system. In mental health, a vertically integrated system of care contracts for a continuum for all ages, program settings, and among different providers. Vertically integrated systems work with providers to ensure appropriate and efficient service delivery. For these efforts, industry analysts estimate vertically integrated systems have cost structures 15% to 50% less than their competitors.

Integrated delivery systems are capable of operating in different reimbursement relationships from a discounted fee for service to a capitated program. Ultimately, providers within the system may operate under differing financial arrangements with the parent organization. True IDSs financially link efficient clinical performance among the members. For example, if the primary care providers are achieving an impressive cost per patient ratio, yet, on further analysis, this is due to their quick referrals to specialists, then the two providers are not financially linked and, therefore, not adequately integrated. The same holds true between the group of practitioners and the hospitals. Successful IDSs hold the *system of providers* accountable for appropriateness of care delivery.

Integrated delivery systems use a variety of legal entities and structures to meet their objectives. They can be organized as for-profit or nonprofit entities. Providers can belong to the system either through direct ownership by the parent organization or as contracted providers. The exact arrangements and structures vary and are reflective of local market needs and local treatment needs and practices. Some systems are organized as MSOs (management service organizations), which can be simple or complex, depending on the functions they serve. Management service organizations are entities that usually contract with practitioner groups, independent practice associations, and medical foundations to provide a range of services required in medical practices, such as accounting, utilization review, and staffing. Another structure includes the staff model HMO, which hires practitioners as salaried employees. Many experts predict an equity-model will develop in most markets because this structure allows practitioners an equity stake in the organization and, therefore, greater commitment and loyalty to the organization. Integrated delivery systems are further discussed in the APA book in the series covering integrated delivery systems.

As these large integrated systems continue to grow, they face the strategic decisions of whether or not to become a risk-bearing entity (an insurer). The system's ability to accept risk for its services and maintain the appropriate reserves as required by state law, will lead to IDSs competing head-on with insurance carriers as they offer behavioral health products in competitive markets. The advantage to becoming an insurance agent is that the IDS would have maximum control of the premium dollar entering the system and therefore greater flexibility in structuring provider reimbursements. However, the differing management skill set, reserves requirements, and licensure are significant barriers to entry.

Should a group practice consider becoming involved in an integrated delivery system? As with other issues in this chapter, financial and clinical practice issues should be considered:

- *Secured Income.* As an IDS group provider, the practice usually receives a guaranteed income source, usually as a capitated payment.
- *Infusion of Capital.* Since the IDS's financial security is tied to that of the practice, the health system may consider contribution of capital to the practice for recruitment, capital purchases, etc.
- *Autonomy of the Group.* Some integrated systems, notably, the "Foundation Model" allow the group to maintain its own integrity. Other groups may be purchased by the IDS, which in itself is often very profitable but may not suit practitioner preference.
- *Access to Covered Lives.* Integrated systems, and most managed care plans in general, offer the practitioner access to enrollees cov-

ered under their plan. As large plans "carve" up local markets, the availability to access selected patient populations becomes smaller and smaller. Thus, one strategy for the group may be strictly a defensive plan to avoid "revenue lockout" by contracting to ensure access to covered lives. Also, IDSs typically have closed provider panels, meaning that they choose providers based on distinct measures of clinical effectiveness. Once the panel is adequate in size to service the covered population, access to the plan's lives becomes nearly impossible.

- *Marketing.* The IDS provides marketing services that may be beyond the means of an individual group practice. As an IDS provider, their successful efforts in publicizing your group as a participating provider may be an added benefit.

- *Provider Profiling.* IDSs may require some type of clinical profiling. Profiling refers to the process of assessing providers' effectiveness by monitoring clinical and cost measures of performance. Typical measures include total costs per patient, length of stay, and recidivism rate. Practitioners should carefully evaluate the system's profiling as potential abuses exist and may need to be dealt with.

- *Provider Qualifications.* How will you represent your practice? What makes your practice valuable to the IDS? If providers in your practice consider themselves specialists, be prepared to document necessary qualifications.

- *Increased MIS Requirements.* One competitive advantage for a delivery system lies in its ability to capture and report relevant information for purchasers, allowing employers to assess effectiveness. This need for information may result in increased MIS costs for your practice.

- *Treatment Protocols.* Protocols are a series of steps designed to offer clinical practice guidelines for an uncomplicated case. Truly integrated systems ensure some standardization of care across the entire treatment continuum and among facilities and providers. If your practice would not consider operating under clinical protocols, an IDS may not be a viable option for the group. Practitioners should recognize that there are helpful protocols and abusive protocols.

As a group considers contracting with integrated systems, it must understand how the reimbursement of providers can affect clinical operations. Again, the key is delivery of appropriate care, using sound clinical judgment, that is sensitive to costs.

Managing the Delivery of Care in Integrated Systems

Vertical integration aligns the incentive system to reward delivery of care at the lowest costs consistent with professional standards. A vertically integrated delivery system is one in which all necessary levels and types of care are available. Multispecialty practices that conduct internal referrals for service are analogous to a vertically integrated system. If the group must go outside the practice to refer patients, the process typically becomes more costly and inconvenient for the patient; treatment also becomes complicated by transfers of records, administrative procedures, etc. The same holds true in vertically integrated systems of care. If a full continuum is offered "in-house," that is, within the IDS's provider panel, the patient can be serviced easier, and costs and treatment modalities can be better managed according to specific criteria (protocols). Standardization of care becomes key. Multispecialty groups that offer a broader range of services, are more attractive to integrative systems because in one contract, they deliver systems that can secure a range of mental health services (resulting in less administrative costs for the system). A system is not integrated if any need is permitted to "fall through the cracks" or requires an ad hoc agreement to be negotiated. In this case, efficiencies are lost. Specialty practices can position themselves well if they understand where they fall on the plan's continuum and how they can fill a hole in the plan's continuum.

To align and standardize clinical practice, most vertically integrated systems rely upon care management processes such as protocols designed by multidisciplinary teams and retrospective analysis of practice pattern statistics to reinforce desired behaviors. One of the most basic behaviors monitored is utilization of the continuum of services to reduce costs.

In behavioral health, the continuum of care may be an extremely complex mix of public, private, and charitable organizations. Table 1 outlines many of the component services in a vertically integrated behavioral health system and the phase at which they are commonly added to the system's continuum. As a group practice, your ability to operate within all modalities in this continuum is a competitive advantage.

TABLE 1   Components of a Vertically Integrated Behavioral Health System

Fee for Service Indemnity Market	Managed/Discounted Indemnity Market	Capitated/At-Risk Managed Market
• Acute care • Residential treatment centers (RTCs) • Outpatient programs	• Partial hospitalization • Day treatment • Crisis intervention • Evening programs	• Telephone triage • Halfway houses/structured living • Community mental health centers • Hospital-based crisis/stabilization centers • Intensive outpatient • Home health care • School counseling centers

Cost Advantages of Integrated Systems

A delivery system in which referrals are made to less expensive providers has a substantial cost advantage over a system where providers do not cooperate with each other to provide care in the least expensive, most appropriate setting. The underlying assumption is that relative costs of different modalities are known to all providers of care within the system and that outcomes are generally equivalent across the continuum.

False economies may be achieved by reducing costs without regard to outcomes. Readmissions and recidivism are especially critical in behavioral health care. An inexpensive treatment modality that frequently fails its clients will not produce cost savings for the delivery system over the long term. Therefore, whenever possible, group practices should work toward a goal of defining and measuring outcomes. New systems are currently available on the market that monitor outcomes across a continuum of providers.

Deliverance of quality care is critically important, especially in risk-sharing contracts. Practitioners that choose to affiliate with managed care organizations (MCOs) and insurers must consider their current compatibility with MCO-style behavioral health care. The simple goal of managing care is to maximize benefit to the patient at minimal cost. Additionally, performance will be compared among peers, which may include professionals substituting for a psychologist's services. In behavioral health, comparison of performance data may be meaningless without severity adjustment. Again, groups of psychologists that can demonstrate an ability to provide measurable outcomes across the entire continuum of service are positioned to maximize their market potential.

Hospital Driven Integration

Many of the vertically integrated delivery systems began with hospital expansion efforts aimed at survival. Over the past decade, hospitals have seen a substantial decline in the inpatient census, partially because of improvements in technology that have supported a shift to ambulatory care, but also driven by Medicare payment reforms and increased utilization monitoring by payers. Seeking to sustain their organizations, many hospitals expanded their services into non-acute care including ambulatory treatment via partial hospitalization, day programs, and outpatient sessions. With these programs, hospitals can shift some fixed and overhead costs as well as staff from the acute setting to generate revenue, reduce losses, and remain solvent and relevant. Under increasing pressure from payers, some hospitals have created psychiatric home health services, on-campus halfway houses, and other innovative services designed to expand the continuum of care towards lower cost alternatives to inpatient care.

Recently, some hospitals have begun to "reach out" to their providers in an effort to increase their loyalty in terms of referrals, bind them contractually, or recognize their importance as channels. Although some of these efforts have been subject to scrutiny from the federal government for antitrust and self-referral issues, others reflect good business sense. Some hospitals have chosen to fund the start-up of MSOs to assist their provider staffs with group purchasing, computer support, billing services, and other administrative practice support as a means of "rewarding" their loyalty.

SUMMARY

This chapter outlined some of the enormous changes occurring in today's mental health market. Market changes cannot be discussed without addressing the redesign and changing reimbursement in behavioral health care. Some practitioners see managed care as a phase, while others believe it to be a permanent economic and clinical phenomenon. Regardless of your conclusion, participation in today's market requires an understanding of the new methods of service delivery and reimbursement. The changing paradigm in health care is this: Treatment decisions are no longer made in isolation; rather, practitioners are increasingly accountable for their services and are reimbursed based on measurable clinical criteria. Integrated systems look for groups that can already deliver the providers and services that can effectively deliver care in that context. Before you look to delivery systems to compete in the market, practitioners should first find the right partners and structure their group practice to enjoy the economies of scale and contracting advantages associated with group affiliation.

Third party reimbursement may or may not be a proportional part of your practice but it will undoubtedly influence your practice in one way or another. With this discussion as a backdrop, the need for and advantages of developing a group practice have been discussed. The next chapter helps practitioners develop a clinical and business format to develop a successful group practice through successful planning.

2

Organizations and Business Planning

L IKE TREATMENT, *developing a practice requires careful planning and analysis. Business planning adheres to the adage that an "ounce of prevention is worth a pound of cure." Before dollars are spent or contracts signed, the practitioner must address some fundamental questions:*

- *Why am I building this practice?*
- *What are my professional goals?*
- *What are my financial goals?*
- *How averse to risk am I?*
- *How will this practice fit in a market of mixed third party and non third party reimbursement?*
- *What changes do I see occurring in the next 5 to 10 years that may affect my decisions now?*
- *How will this system reflect my personal goals?*

This chapter introduces key steps in the process of organizing a practice, including defining a group vision and assessing the feasibility of the group practice. This chapter culminates with a sample format for a business plan, focusing on the cultural, operational, financial, and marketing issues relevant to successful practice development.

GOALS AND OBJECTIVES

All operational planning ultimately originates from a set of agreed upon goals and objectives for the organization. Specifically, early in the formation process, solo practitioners and group members decide questions of:

- professional development among clinicians
- desired income levels
- ability to deliver needed services

Once set, all future decisions stem from supporting the collective vision for the practice. Therefore, expression of dissenting opinions is encouraged at this stage so that they may be worked through. Potential partners explore their compatibility—are their goals able to be accommodated or are they mutually exclusive? Is one practitioner's desire to share risk among other partners at odds with other colleagues' needs for clinical autonomy? As specific needs are verbalized, it may become obvious that two practitioners with mutually exclusive visions for the practice may not move forward with the undertaking. It is best to establish "success" criteria early on rather than have a member attempt to change the rules after the organizational structure is completed.

Potential partners usually have multiple motives for group development, which typically fall into one of three major categories, as Table 2 illustrates. What are your motivations?

The practice will be developed organizationally, clinically, and financially as defined by the shared vision for practice success. It becomes part of your entity's *written* "mission statement." A sample mission statement may read like this:

> The Main Street Clinic, a multispecialty family therapy group practice, assists patients afflicted by family crises and provides measurable, quality, and cost-sensitive services to payers of behavioral health care.

In writing a mission statement, answer who you are ("Main Street Clinic, a multispecialty family therapy group practice") and what you do ("assists, provides"—action words, active voice.) Additionally, if the statement does not become too cumbersome, state *why this is important*. A clear and concise mission statement provides the guiding principles for practice formation and becomes, in effect, the group's "rallying cry."

EXPLORING THE FEASIBILITY

The central questions regarding the feasibility of a practice include:

1. As a group, are we compatible both clinically and in our personal ambitions for this practice?
2. Is there a market for our services that will support our personal ambitions?

At this point in the merger or development process, a sense of commitment and good faith naturally develops among the members. Cultures,

TABLE 2   Reasons for Group Practice Development

Benefits to the Members	• Better practice coverage • Ability to take worry-free vacations • Shared financial liability • Consultations on complex cases • Professional interaction • Maintenance of a better library through shared resources • Ability to practice more within a chosen specialty • More predictable working hours • Stable income • Better retirement plan
Improved Practice Management	• Employment of more specialized or skilled personnel (family therapist, professional manager, etc.) • More efficient use of existing personnel/office space • Better use of office space through staggered hours • Ability to move to a larger facility • Pooled staffing resources • Shared costs for equipment, space, etc.
Benefits to the Patients/Clients	• Greater patient access to more community practitioners • More resources/expertise on-site • Improved continuity of care in the absence of one clinician • Greater practice diversity

staffs, assets, and operations must be examined to determine their ability to unite and become a single functioning entity. "Letters of intent" may be developed to formalize this process and to prevent misunderstandings. Five areas typically dictate both the *cultural and the financial* feasibility of merging as a group practice: assets/liabilities, practitioner compensation, governance structure, administration, and retirement planning.

Assets/Liabilities

Although a subjective judgment, the simplest scenario involves practices of equal net value where solo practitioners join together with equal financial risk at stake. This is rarely the case, however. Assessing and determining value assigned to a partner's practice can be a difficult undertaking. Often, hiring a health care consultant to assess a partner's practice is the most efficient and objective means. Among the issues to consider with your consultant:

1. What should be included in evaluating assets and liabilities?
2. How will the valuation be performed and how will members fund this exercise?
3. Are there contingent liabilities or personal debts involved and how will these be considered?
4. Can compensation arrangements in the first few years of the practice be arranged to alter or make up for imbalances in assets and liabilities?
5. What value will the members of the practice place on reputation, clientele, and goodwill?

Practice Development Tip: **An often asked question is how many practitioners are needed to build a successful group practice. No answer exists for this question since the vision of the group and marketplace needs and demands will dictate the group's size. A good rule of thumb is to have as many practitioners as will support the group's mission.**

Practitioner Compensation

Members need to settle this issue up-front as it is conceivably a deal-breaker. Practitioners develop an understanding of each other's income needs. Members must be concrete and specific regarding expected compensation: concessions are likely to be necessary. Consider hiring an outside third party to assist in modeling potential compensation and ensure the consultant accounts for the group's start-up or merger costs. Expect the greatest challenges on compensation issues to come from established, successful practitioners.

Governance Structure

Except for solo practices and some partnership forms, all entities require a board of directors, executive committee, and key officers. Critical to this process is establishing the limits of their authority and their role in decisions for the practice. For which issues will they become the decision-making authority? How will key leaders be monitored and evaluated? New business opportunities and managed care contracts may test authority limits. A governance structure rooted in member buy-in and consensus building will delay responsiveness to the market. See chapter 6 for a further discussion of this important topic.

Administration and Support Staff

At least one advantage to a merger is the economies of scale offered by a shared staff. Practitioners naturally become comfortable working daily with their respective support personnel and managers. Often, a spouse may take an active role in running the business. Yet, as multiple practices come together, staffs must inevitably also merge. Members must decide up-front how this merging of the staffs and consolidation of resources will occur.

Retirement Issues

Members need to address their retirement plans and decide how the practice will fund their collective (and individual) retirement goals. Depending on the age of the practitioners in question, sources of retirement income and funding of a retirement plan can be another potential deal-breaker. Look for practitioners that share similar goals for retirement income and similar strategies for how to get there.

Decision: Develop a Single or Multispecialty Group Practice?

The feasibility of a group practice is often determined when members focus on whether services will be single or multispecialty. However, deciding whether to develop a single or multispecialty group is contingent on the business makeup of group members, the market's managed care penetration, and the collective group goals. For clarity, the terms single and multispecialty are defined as they refer to group practices:

- *Single Specialty*—A practice dedicated to the treatment of a single diagnosis or a single group of ailments, such as schizophrenic disorders, anxiety disorders, etc. Single specialty groups may service adult, child, and adolescent populations.
- *Multispecialty*—A practice dedicated to the treatment of multiple diagnoses. Multispecialty groups typically offer the services required for comprehensive treatment of an illness to discourage outside referral. Some multispecialty groups integrate with physician groups.

In a tightly managed market (high managed care penetration) or a market dominated by delivery systems, payers seek to lower their administrative costs by contracting with groups of providers or systems of care whenever possible. A *multispecialty group in this market holds significant competitive advantage over a single specialty* practice because, in one contract, the payer can lock-in the services of many practitioners serving multiple diagnoses. The payer would bear significantly more administrative costs to contract separately with a comparable number of single specialty practices. Multispecialty practices offer payers a "one stop shopping" advantage, not only for contracting but for utilization review (UR) services and quality assurance. In short, there are fewer clinical procedures to monitor and therefore lower administrative costs. The fewer the contracted entities, the lower is the administrative burden, which ultimately increases the payer's competitiveness. Therefore, in tight managed care markets, multispecialty groups would expect to have the upper hand in negotiations.

In tightly managed markets, multispecialty groups hold a significant competitive advantage over single specialty groups.

For these same reasons, single specialty groups are disadvantaged in markets with significant managed care unless the group is a niche player. This means that the group is either the only provider or one of a few providers of service such that competition between groups is minimal. Though possible in some markets, the group must discern whether this advantage is *sustainable*. How long can the single specialty group offer services before competition is offered from other single or multispecialty groups?

It may be possible to draw competitive advantage on the basis of price or quality. Competitive advantage on a quality basis is sometimes difficult to project since it is usually based on buyer (i.e., payer) perception. If the group's cost structure is such that it can engage in aggressive pricing against other groups, this may be an effective short-term strategy. However, the single specialty group will still be under pressure from multispecialty groups that offer all-in-one pricing for multiple diagnoses.

Single or multispecialty group practices competing for contracts may consider, as a strategy, integration with primary care physicians (internists, family practitioners, OB-GYNs, and pediatricians). In medical/surgical systems, the primary care physician (PCP) is the "gatekeeper" to the system, that is, the PCP controls referrals to the more costly specialists. This is a typical way HMOs control costs by driving treatment to the least costly but most efficient level of care. However, a large percentage of PCPs are called upon to treat mental and behavioral health and substance abuse conditions without having the training to properly treat and diagnose mental and behavioral illnesses. In some cases, psychological problems are manifested with physiological symptoms. Without significant behavioral health care training, PCPs may either misdiagnose, prescribe an inappropriate treatment, or refer to a specialist that may not be required. This is not deliberate—however, it is a fact that primary care physicians are currently treating and sending patients within the delivery system without training as a mental health/substance abuse(MH/SA) professional. In such cases, the psychologist is a more appropriate practitioner to diagnose and treat behavioral health patients. If office treatment is not possible, the psychologist is also the appropriate gatekeeper to correctly refer patients to the proper modality in the behavioral health system. This setup serves the PCP well by ensuring correct care in the correct modality as well as supplying access to the MCO's covered lives for the group practice.

Practice Development Tip: Look for opportunities to control access to mental health systems. In this way, psychologists can position themselves as "gatekeepers" of systems of care.

In markets with few systems of care, the option of developing a single or multispecialty group practice is much less one-sided. In this market, we assume that most patients are private pay patients who pay all costs for service. Therefore, as a practitioner, the financial incentive is to maintain or expand market share (which expands the revenue base). The notion of owning a single or multispecialty group practice in this market is largely invisible to the private pay patient—buyers are not necessarily concerned with the "one stop shopping" notion so important to managed care payers. In fact, in this market, quality may be very difficult to communicate; it may be recognized in the professional community but not necessarily perceived by payers. Therefore, the decision for building a single or multispecialty practice in markets with little or no managed care is largely one of practice preference. In this market, consider the following guidelines:

- From a business perspective, single or multispecialty group practices share administrative support staff and thus lower overhead costs.
- Single practices hold a competitive advantage if they provide unique (niche) services. Success can be achieved if the practice is considered a "center of excellence," recognized as such by customers and other practitioners. Be careful though—quality is a perception made by customers and requires additional marketing efforts to communicate.
- Multispecialty practices offer an opportunity to control referrals and expand the scope of the practice to reach new markets.
- Reputation of the practitioners may be an additional source of competitive advantage.

Thus, in tight managed care markets, multispecialty groups offer the competitive advantages most sought after by commercial payers. In other markets with no managed care, either group can meet with success, although competitive advantage as a single specialty group may be difficult to sustain. Make your decision based not on the current state of the market, but on your most accurate projection of the future penetration of managed care and needs of employers. Build a practice that services current needs but is easily adaptable to a changing health care environment.

DEVELOPING AND IMPLEMENTING A BUSINESS PLAN

Develop a business plan for the new practice or potential merger. Proactive care in preparing a detailed business plan for practice development and ongoing operations may pay great dividends, including securing potential investors or other practitioners. For example, most investors will require comprehensive plans that consider challenges to early success and contingency planning for such circumstances. An outline of a business plan customized for use in practice development is included in this chapter as a model.

At this point, read through the sample business plan (see appendix to this chapter) and try to envision how the final document will look. You probably cannot and should not develop a comprehensive document at this time, but the group should begin to understand what issues will be easily addressed and which issues will be difficult and require outside assistance. As you read through this book, come back to this chapter and continue to add detail to the business plan. Remember: Plan for and control your practice's destiny. Here is the place to start that formal process.

IMPLEMENTATION AND FOLLOW-UP

Each implementation and follow-up experience is different. However, one of the most important issues is understanding contingency planning. Investors, insurers, and others will want to know, "If the assumptions made in your business plan do not occur in reality, what is your plan?" Planning for contingencies is often an exhausting process in the business planning cycle and is frequently overlooked. However, it is absolutely critical to eliminate as many unforeseen occurrences as possible early on and establish a mechanism to deal with them. This is particularly true for any and all assumptions about market trends and rates of managed care penetrations. For example: If it was predicted that capitated contracting would comprise only 10% of the core business in year 2 and, in fact, it represents over 50% percent, how will this organization manage the unplanned-for shift in business revenue? As an example of the latter, how will the organization react if revenues in years 2 and 3 are below financial projections? Contingencies should be developed for both favorable and unfavorable scenarios. There may be an occasion when profitability increases faster than projected. How will the timetable, as outlined in the plan, be affected?

Practice Development Tip: *Your business plan will appear more credible if contingency planning is detailed and conducted in earnest.*

SUMMARY

This chapter began the process of assessing the fit of two organizations considering a group merger. Here, we laid the foundation for further discussion of group formation issues in chapter 3. Without developing a clear sense of vision and assessment of compatibility, other structural issues become more difficult to resolve. The business plan was deliberately presented early in the text to help readers see up-front the issues required for planning. Business plans should be living documents—they are most effective when they continually reflect new developments in the planning process. It is not too early to try working through a first draft. The document will become clearer as the group continues developing its shared vision and works through other important structural issues presented later in this text.

APPENDIX
SAMPLE OUTLINE: BUSINESS PLAN

1. Introduction
   - Name of the business.
   - Form of business entity (e.g., partnership, limited liability corporation, regular corporation, S corporation).
   - Name and address of primary point of contact for questions regarding this business plan.
   - One paragraph summary of your purpose for this enterprise (including a succinct communication of market needs you will serve).
   - If you are planning a merger, briefly summarize the two organizations' strengths, weakness, profitability, and reason for a "fit" between the two.
   - Summarize capital requirements.
   - Discuss the goal of the entity.
   - What is the group's mission statement?
   - Briefly, how is success in this organization to be measured?

2. Industry Analysis: What factors are motivating this venture?
   - Discuss industry trends, including managed care, shifting of risk, market consolidation, and development of integrated systems.
   - What is the industry size and projected growth rate? Discuss nationally and regionally. Be very specific in defining market size.
   - Make reasonable predictions about market trends.
   - Discuss the impact of recent state and federal legislation and its potential impact on the practice.
   - Perform a thorough managed care analysis of the current market area. Focus on degree of penetration, payer mix, development of integrated systems, percentages of risk-sharing contracts, requirements for outcomes data, etc. Explain how the entity will address these issues.

- Assess the managed care market in 2 to 3 years, if possible. Discuss any relevant trends specific to the local area that may affect decision making.

3. The Management Team
   - Identify key management personnel, qualifications (resumes) to manage the entity, experience, and plans to integrate the management and clinical expertise of the practice.
   - Organizational chart, if applicable. Show key positions and staff personnel.
   - Discuss the entity's compensation plan.
   - Identify the Board of Directors/Executive Committee/Trustees as applicable. Discuss their qualifications. Discuss their level of authority and degree of participation in practice dynamics. How will the entity maintain or increase their level of understanding of current mental health issues.
   - Identify key supporting expertise including consultants, lawyers, tax advisers, and CPAs.

4. The Clinical Services
   - Discuss the group's treatment philosophy.
   - Describe the entity's quality assurance program including UR, case management, clinical protocols, and outcomes measurement.
   - Discuss your contracting strategy. Who do you contract with? What kinds of payment mechanisms are accepted?
   - Discuss the ability of the clinicians (and staff) to operate profitably in a risk-sharing environment.
   - Discuss the importance of customer satisfaction and the implementation of surveys.
   - Discuss the decision to develop the entity as either a single-specialty, a multispecialty, or a multidisciplinary group and how this decision is supported by either financial need or effective market positioning.
   - Discuss location of the practice, building space (lease/purchase?), office space and staffing, etc.

5. The Marketing Plan
   - Describe and clearly define the entity's market. Discuss geo-

graphic size (a map may be helpful here) and potential market growth.

- Identify the customers (patients and payers). Classify market potential according to payer mix and reimbursement methodology (fee for service, capitation, etc.). Develop an alternate classification by diagnoses, if possible.
- Discuss strategies to segment and target a specific groups in the market. (With fixed resources, namely time and money, to spend on marketing efforts—where will the practice get the most "bang for the buck"?)
- Include a copy of your marketing plan.
- Who is the competition?
- What is the distinct competitive advantage that differentiates the entity from its competitors (quality, reputation, etc.) How do you communicate this to the target market?
- Discuss the marketing mix, including:

  - *Company.* What are the organization's strengths and weaknesses?
  - *Customers.* Who are they, what do they want in behavioral health services.
  - *Competition.* What are their strengths and weaknesses? Their probable courses of action in response to a new entity?
  - *Price.* What is the fee schedule and how is it derived? What is the plan for profitability analysis of capitated contracts? Bundled pricing?
  - *Place.* Where will the main office be located? Are there satellite offices?
  - *Promotion.* How will your services be communicated? By what medium? By whom? What will this cost? Projected benefit?

- Discuss how the organization will manage customer complaints.

6. The Financial Plan (with assistance of a qualified CPA/consultant)
   - Pro forma income statements projected out to three years.
   - Pro forma balance sheets projected out to three years.

- Cash flow analysis, paying particular attention to retained earnings which are especially important when contracting on a risk-sharing basis.
- Break-even analysis, modeled under varying assumptions. (clearly articulate these assumptions).
- Schedule of capital requirements including short term (less than one year), mid-term (years 1-2), and longer term (year 3 and beyond).
- Indicate mechanisms for securing necessary capital.

7. Contingency Planning and Risk Management
    - Identify points in the plan that are subject to change.
    - Project verbally (and financially) how this will affect the practice.
    - Explain the contingency plan(s).

8. Appendixes—Supporting Documents
    - Partnership agreements, articles of incorporation
    - Applicable licenses
    - Contracts with other health organizations
    - Insurance policies
    - Marketing materials
    - Resumes

3

Group Dynamics—Developing a Vision

M ANY GROUP PRACTICES *fail when there is not sufficient understanding of the resources and level of commitment necessary for success. Why do some practices flourish and become financially stable while others flounder? This chapter explores
in greater detail the importance of a shared vision to practice success.
As psychologists, your knowledge and understanding of group dynamics will have invaluable applications to the formation of the group practice.*

*Every practitioner has specific needs or motivations when joining
a group practice. As the practice grows, individual behavior is affected
by group interaction. Conflicts inevitably develop and are resolved.
Decision making gains complexity. As relationships develop that will
determine livelihood and income, practice culture and therapeutic philosophy become critical to group survival, contentment, and profitability. This chapter relates the basics of organizational dynamics to the
behavioral health professional's environment. If the group is profitable
but cannot resolve conflict, it will fail. The best way to resolve conflict
is to understand its source and how you can plan for potential problems.*

*The objective of this chapter is twofold: first, to provide a theoreti-
cal understanding of group behavior to help shape the group formation
process, and second, strategies to maximize individual strengths and minimize conflicts that threaten the practice. The chapter concludes with a
discussion of salary issues, a frequent source of tension among new
groups.*

DEVELOPING A VISION

This chapter is not simply an academic exercise in group dynamics but
rather is designed to increase provider awareness of individual needs and
cultural fit of merging practitioners. Two groups or practitioners who have

strategically different goals, one financial and the other clinical for example, *can* merge as a successful group practice. However, individual needs must be addressed up-front to effectively deal with them in later business planning. Good working groups rarely "just happen": synergies are not always naturally developed. Successful groups *create* synergies by creating environments of shared goals and resources and by recognizing the merging of separate cultures.

All group practices are the merger of two practices. For example, when two practices each with three practitioners decide to affiliate, the merger that results integrates two distinct staffs and cultures. Yet, the same dynamics occur between two solo practitioners. It should be noted that while there may be other ways to conceptualize group behavior than the one presented here, this model has proven to be quite useful in a business context. As a sole practitioner, you undoubtedly have a small staff and perhaps one or two associates to assist you in running the practice and treating patients. As the two soloists affiliate, a merger is still consummated— the two solo practices and staffs, each with their own distinct cultures, blend to become one functioning unit. For this reason, principles of group dynamics apply to either situation.

Why People Form Groups

Groups have such tremendous influence on individual behavior that a brief study of group behavior is appropriate. As two practices merge, you must consider individual practitioner needs for group affiliation. Are they comparable among the two groups or will there always be some unresolved and unspoken void between practitioner's goals? Individuals affiliate in groups to satisfy certain needs as outlined below:

- *Security.* Security may be the biggest reason for group practice formation. Without being surrounded by a group of colleagues, many practitioners feel the pressure of standing alone. Being a member of a group helps develop a forum to share both ideas and business risk. New groups, for example, often look for the security of belonging to a system of care where the referral base is secure through contracting with a managed care organization. New associates may require the security of affiliating with an established practice while their own practice styles develop. Security is the driving force behind much of the consolidation among providers and insurers in the medical and mental health industries.

- *Social Needs.* Some practitioners may choose to affiliate with a group in order to work with a trusted colleague, spouse, or friend. In these cases, the desire for social interaction as a group is a major motivator behind group formation.
- *Esteem.* Affiliation with a renowned or highly respected practice fulfills group and individual needs for esteem. From a purely business perspective, the opportunity to "piggy back" off a developed reputation has obvious advantages but the need to be compared in the same circle with established and respected practitioners should not be overlooked.
- *Proximity Needs.* Groups of practitioners may merge or individuals may develop a practice simply for the convenience of their respective locations. Often, they desire to take advantage of marketing opportunities in serving a local clientele. Proximity affects individual lifestyle (shorter commuting distance, opportunity to become part of a local community) and therefore fulfills many practitioners' need for association.
- *Group Goals.* Groups affiliate when there are shared group goals. For example, two groups may merge when there is a common treatment philosophy. Caution is advised in making association decisions on this basis as perceptions, attitudes, personality, and learning may affect group goals.
- *Economic Motivations.* Practices may develop or merge strictly for economic reasons. The two groups agree at the outset about the value placed on economic advancement relative to other motivations.

THE LIFE CYCLE OF A GROUP PRACTICE

Groups typically affiliate according to four stages of development as illustrated in Figure 1. In stage one, two individuals or groups move to gain some mutual acceptance. This may be motivated by one practitioner either expressing an interest to affiliate or exploring another party's interest in a group venture. At this stage, the parties develop a mutual understanding of each other's practice goals without becoming encumbered by the details. If successful in this stage, a certain acceptance and trust between the two groups develops. Ask yourself, "Is this an individual I would want to practice with and have my income, security, and other needs dependent on?" Intuition is critical at this point.

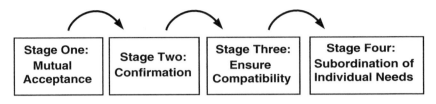

FIGURE 1   Four stages of group formation.

In the next stage, stage two, groups typically move forward in their discussions and expand the range of issues. It is still an information-collecting stage. No decisions to form have been made, but different individuals from each practice are looking for further information to verify or contradict the opinions developed earlier. At this point, each group assesses the possible cultural compatibility between the practices. Sample questions that are addressed include, "What is your practice's treatment philosophy for bipolar disorder?" or "What are your plans for further development of this practice?"

At stage two, group members also give serious consideration to personality issues that may explode later if left unexplored. Do individuals feel they can practice together? Would you trust the care of your patient to another practitioner in the group? Can you reach compromise on important group practice decisions with this person? Do you respect this practitioner's approach to patient treatment? Are there any integrity issues? Is respect mutual?

Stage three of group formation is a further extension of stage two except that compatibility issues become more focused, direct, and technical to identify and resolve potential "show stoppers." With cultural fit assessed in stage two, stage three involves technical compatibility around such issues as financial management, governance, and clinical practice issues. Issues like strategic direction, compensation, and benefits must be resolved at this time.

Technical compatibility may be a difficult issue for a practice to resolve—money, time, and practice patterns are sensitive issues to most clinicians. Cultural issues will eventually fade as the newly formed practice creates its own distinct, unique culture. But technical issues routinely surface as the practice takes on other partners, enters new contracts, and expands to new markets and services. Your ability to enter into and resolve these issues may reflect on the group's future ability to address these and other delicate issues. As the group continues to merge, a level of trust develops between the two parties. If this does not happen, ask yourself why? How difficult was it to work through tough issues? Are both groups unable to compromise now and is this an indication of the practice's future?

The final stage in group formation occurs when group goals overtake individual goals. This may occur months after the official entity is developed and is often characterized by the development of single cultural norms. The norms of the previous independent practices become subordinate to the larger organization's.

Why is this important to the practitioner? Generally, you may consider the group to be developing normally if these stages occur in some sequence. However, if a group immediately jumps to stages three and four, this may be an indication that more fundamental issues have been omitted—issues that *will* need to be addressed at a less opportune time. Practitioners frequently ask, "How long will it take to form a group?" There is no magical time for group formation to occur, as it is a function of how much the merging parties initially differ. If their clinical practices, compensation goals, management styles, group norms, and structure, to name a few, are incompatible, all the planning in the world may not make for a successful affiliation. If the differences are few, group practice can take place in relatively quick order. The size of the two practices may also contribute to the speed of formation. In general, two groups of three to four practitioners each that generally agree in principle to the issues outlined in this text should consider 3 to 6 months as a "ballpark" figure.

CHARACTERISTICS OF GROUPS THAT AFFECT GROUP FORMATION

Over time, groups develop unique characteristics that define themselves. Some characteristics are written, others are unwritten but nonetheless important in defining the group. As your practice continues to form, consider the influence of structure, roles, and norms as potential influences on group development or merger. As you consider these phenomena, how can you structure the practice to ease potential conflicts and maximize the separate strengths brought by each player? Where applicable, the following sections pose questions and strategies to consider.

Structure

When strategists refer to organizational structure, images of pyramidal organizational charts quickly come to mind. Certainly, they are useful tools in describing the organization's hierarchy to the outside world. Groups may develop an *unwritten* hierarchy based in anything the group finds of value. If a particular practitioner attended an executive MBA program and displays superior finance and accounting skills, that member will achieve a status for financial management issues that is not afforded other members. The same holds true for other skill sets. Effective groups identify those unwritten skills that lend structure to the organization and establish a governance or operating environment that recognizes individual strengths. In many cases, status differences create power bases and an informal hierarchy within the group. The group's formal structure does not always define the actual hierarchy and power bases of the group.

The larger the practice and more complex its services, the greater is the need to provide structure to the group. As two diverse practices merge, providers must inevitably face structural issues not present as separate, smaller practices. Will informal leaders now be required to assume more active roles in practice management? The new entity must develop a formal structure that leverages individual strength. In cases where two practitioners share a certain expertise, look to leverage their collective strengths by structuring governance and group responsibilities to allow them to work collaboratively. If a particularly necessary skill set is lacking, this may warrant further efforts to recruit an associate that fills the void.

Status Hierarchy

Status may be achieved due to seniority, practice excellence, reputation, or a particular skill set. How will internal group dynamics adjust to a new associate who lacks the experience to command any clinical status from the group? Will this member forever be subordinate to all members of the organization on all practice issues? How can the associate be integrated and afforded some status that might "level the playing field" and prevent group dysfunction. One possibility may be to let a new associate represent all associates at board meetings or before the executive committee.

An individual's status in the practice may be a source of potential conflict or, in the worst case, contribute to group dysfunction. If, for example, the most senior practitioner in the group is allowed to drive all decisions by virtue of his/her seniority, this may create ill-feelings and possibly poor outcomes for the practice. The issues may interfere with sound decisions made by personnel empowered to do so.

Roles

Roles, or organized sets of behavior, may be defined according to three possibilities:

- expected roles (expected behavior)
- perceived roles (behaviors a person *believes* should be enacted)
- enacted roles (actual behavior)

Conflict occurs when there is a difference in any of the three roles among members. For example, if a group of clinicians verbally empowers Dr. Jones to manage the business affairs of the practice, there may develop an incongruence between Dr. Jones' expected and perceived roles. In this case, the clinicians *expect* Dr. Jones to be a business manager. However, Dr. Jones perceives his role to be that of both clinician *and* administrator. Suppose, to continue this example, Dr. Jones is remiss in his administrative duties but continues his excellent work with patients. In this case, there is a conflict between expected roles and enacted roles since Dr. Jones is *expected* to be both a clinician and a manager but, in fact, only performs (enacts) his clinical functions. This example of incongruence among expected, perceived, and enacted roles is a subject dealt with by psychologists every day with patients. Roles within the new organization should be carefully defined to manage all members' understanding of each other's roles.

Practice Development Tip: Manage role conflict by ensuring that each person's role in the organization is well defined and articulated. While this may change over time, one of the quickest ways for a developing group practice to get stuck is if practitioners do not clearly define each member's role in the organization.

Creation of a new practice also creates new roles for individual practitioners. Ensure that governance structures do not further create role conflict for members. Key to role resolution is a clear understanding of each individual's role in the organization and open communication when conflicts arise. As you develop your organization, are you creating potential

role conflicts? Do practitioners understand each other's roles in the organization? Have they been formally acknowledged and agreed upon? As in
the above example, clarification of roles is important especially in the early
stages of group formation.

---

*Practice Development Tip: When several solo or group
practices are developing a new group practice, it is often
useful for the parties to invest a day or two at the other
group's practice to experience the daily routine with
patients and staff members and observe how unwritten
norms affect the practice's management and structure.*

Norms

Norms are frequently a source of conflict among merged groups. Each
practice brings its own set of written and unwritten standards to the merger
and, very often, these are in direct conflict with each other. Norms may
develop for dress, conduct, evaluation of members, and other reasons. For
example: One group bases increased compensation on the number of new
referrals and contribution margin of the individual while another group
compensates strictly on seniority. How will the groups resolve this issue?
Written norms are easier to compromise. Unwritten norms, however, define a practice's culture and are difficult to verbalize but, rather, must be
experienced. Two parties interested in a merger should invest a day or two
at the other group's practice to experience the daily routine with patients
and staff members and observe how unwritten norms affect the practice's
management and structure. Are these differences, if any, insurmountable?

Norms are standards of behavior that are a result of group member
interaction over time. As two groups merge, expect the norms of each
separate group to become subordinate to newly developed and shared
norms. Notice in the definition that norms are developed *over time*. This
implies that the group's leadership begins early to shape and influence
desired group behavior before norms develop by default (which may be
contrary to the practice's vision). For example, if the new group considers
its goal to contract with managed care, how can standards of behavior be
shaped early on to manage the treatments and costs of behavioral health
care? Group leaders may, for instance, establish treatment protocols as a

possible response. The point is that norms are easier to create and shape early in the formation process and difficult to undo later.

Leadership

Like written and unwritten norms, there are recognized and unrecognized leaders that exert power in an organization. Organizational charts may tell the world a practice's management structure but they do not necessarily reflect real leadership. In a partnership where members have equal financial risk, is there one practitioner that others rely upon for leadership? Is this due to a personal leadership style, dominant personality, or recognition of a certain status? Do members of the potential merging practice exert leadership at certain times and in conjunction with their specific expertise? If so, who guides this group of leaders? As you build your group practice, who seems to emerge as the unspoken leader? Who embodies the goals of the group and typically voices their concerns? Who does the group trust to resolve internal conflicts? This person (or people) is key to organizational success and you. Target them early to influence the formation process and help achieve member buy-in.

Cohesiveness

Generally, groups become more cohesive when they share similar needs in a satisfactory manner. Cohesion can occur at different levels in the organization. Are the less-senior practitioners a cohesive group yet the practice is fragmented as a unit? Does a cohesive practice ostracize new members for an unnecessarily long time? In a merger, does one cohesive practice have difficulty integrating with the other practice? As you look to reshape the new group's norms, be aware that cohesive groups are typically reluctant to give up their well developed patterns of behavior. Cohesiveness among groups is only an asset when it results in shared norms that support the group's identity and goals.

An understanding of group dynamics can help alleviate potential problems of the new practice. Though there is no "checklist" to consult when dealing with these issues, this does not understate their importance. Assessing the fit of two practices and developing norms to deal with conflict often separate success from failure. Group practice development is like any other linking of two parties—both bring certain strengths and weaknesses to the relationship and without a "fit," the relationship begins on shifting sand.

In some cases, group characteristics can be shaped by defining how the organization will be structured. In many cases, however, formal organizations can disrupt the natural synergies that develop over time and ultimately lead to high performance teams. It is enough for the practitioners developing a group practice to understand that differences between two groups invariably exist and that an awareness of potential conflicts in and of themselves will help the two groups merge as a single, cohesive unit.

RECOGNIZING AND MANAGING CONFLICT IN THE GROUP PRACTICE

Whenever individuals work together, conflicts inevitably result. Not all conflict is bad for the group—it is often a healthy forum for solving disputes and provides a platform to further develop group cohesion (on successful resolution). Yet, some conflicts become bitter and can destroy the group. Conflicts are best resolved when their nature can be determined or avoided and mechanisms exist to deal with them as they surface. This section introduces sources of conflict and several strategies for their resolution.

Role Conflict

Role conflict occurs when members are required to perform multiple functions in the organization. *Person–role conflict* occurs in a practice when responsibilities of a practitioner are in conflict with that person's attitudes, values, or morals. Defense lawyers frequently experience role conflict when they are required to defend a self-confessed criminal. *Intrarole conflict* develops when different individuals define a clinician's role with different expectations. The conflict occurs when the individual feels he cannot satisfy the requirements of either party. *Interrole conflict* occurs when a practitioner is placed in multiple roles, each with different expectations. Again, practitioner–managers are prone to this conflict due to the many "hats" they wear—clinician, office manager, manager care negotiator, supervisor, etc. How can the merger of two organizations avoid this conflict? How can the groups balance their expectations to ensure that practitioners can successfully perform in multiple roles?

Interdependence

Interdependence is an issue all merging groups must face and overcome. In general, interdependence issues arise when one group depends on another to perform its tasks. Interdependence can take three different forms:

- *Pooled Interdependence*—occurs when parties operate independently but the results of their operations dictate the success of the organization. Two psychological practices that do not integrate their clinical staffs may be prone to conflict. This issue is partially resolved by creating integrated delivery systems where financial performance is hinged on the performance of the entire entity delivering cost-effective care. No one organization (hospital, group practice, MCO) can achieve financial excellence on its own—success depends on the pooled or collective, integrated performance of the entire entity.

  In group practice, there are two ways to overcome this conflict. First, in a multispecialty practice with differing lines of business, organizational goals and compensation can be structured to ensure a coordinated contribution. In single specialty groups, establishment of clinical protocols and increased interaction of all clinical staff in the services delivery process may minimize conflict.

- *Sequential Interdependence*—occurs when one party must complete its task before another can begin and complete the task. This can occur between clinicians and frequently occurs between clinicians and staff. For example, the receptionist must schedule the visit with the necessary practitioner before treatment can begin. Initial testing and assessment must occur before a treatment plan is established. This conflict is overcome in the group practice by implementing clinical protocols and process flow diagrams illustrating the importance of each member's responsibility for service delivery. The process of effective service delivery breaks down if any members fail to complete their respective tasks. The receptionist must schedule the patient and draw the necessary medical record prior to the therapist performing a testing procedure. The therapist must complete the diagnosis before an effective treatment can begin. As a group practice, learn to recognize what steps must be performed sequentially and ensure that staff have the time and other resources to perform them to prevent backlogging of patients.

- *Reciprocal Interdependence* —occurs when one member's outcome from a process is another's input. The interaction between a psychologist and another mental health provider is an example of this type of interdependence. Here the psychologist makes a diagnosis and refers internally to another provider, as appropriate. The social worker receives information about the patient's family, living or work conditions and then makes necessary arrangements for follow-up care or assistance.

Interdependence issues are very real in group formation, particularly among established and successful groups. Managing the delivery of care in integrated systems requires the group to squeeze efficiencies from its internal operations. Interdependence requires all members to understand their assigned function in the group and to further understand how their performance affects the performance of the entire group. For the solo practitioner entering group practice for the first time, the interdependence among the staff and providers may be a new adjustment.

Differences in Goals

When two distinct practices are merged, there must be some commonality in the new group's goals. Conflicts develop when goals are not compatible and, often, the use of scarce resources such as administrative staff can lead to conflict. At least one major advantage of forming a group practice is the economies of scale created in sharing administrative overhead. When goals are disjointed, limited resources like staff, money, and time must be allocated one way or the other to support one group's values. It becomes a "zero-sum" situation where one party benefits at the other's expense.

Conflict Resolution

Group practices have a number of techniques available to help resolve group conflicts. Note that each potential solution is not necessarily applicable in every situation but depends largely on the complexity of the conflict.

- *Problem Solving*—face to face meetings to clarify misunderstandings. Confrontation style management requiring effective one-on-one communication skills. Problem solving is quite effective at resolving the root of the issue but a person with good personnel skills is necessary to make it work.
- *Superordinate Goals*—development of higher goals whose successful accomplishment requires cooperation of all levels of the group. May be most useful for role conflict resolution.
- *Expansion of Resources*—making more resources available to prevent internal competition and conflict due to limited resources. May be an acceptable method as it generally satisfies the parties in conflict; however, it is subject to limitations on resources and may have a potential for abuse.
- *Avoidance*—at best, a short term solution. Generally not recommended for group practices that require a high level of staff interaction and clinical coordination.
- *Compromise*—traditional method that suffers in that neither party is truly satisfied. May require third party intervention when the conflicting groups or members are particularly divided.
- *Authoritative Command*—most successful in short term conflict resolution or when time-sensitive decisions are required. Empowers one individual to make a decision on resolving the conflict with which two parties will agree. Typically, this method does not promote group cohesion but may be effective in certain situations.
- *Identifying a Common Enemy*—similar to developing a superordinate goal. Helps the parties to focus on something outside of the immediate area of concern.

Conflict typically arises over the issue of compensation. Therefore, with the above strategies for conflict resolution in mind, issues of income relevant to the group practice are discussed as an example.

Conflict Resolution Example: Practitioner Compensation

No one compensation system works for every group practice. Some practices may prefer to keep practitioners as salaried employees while others prefer to base salary on measures of either individual or group production. Other groups may choose to assign a lower base salary and offer large bonuses that depend on some incentive-based plan. This section offers ideas for determining practitioner compensation. As you read this section, be aware of both the positive and the possible negative consequences of distributing income. Whenever applicable, these consequences will be highlighted.

Salary Versus Compensation

Salary and compensation must first be clearly defined and the terms should not be misused with practitioners. Salary represents a fixed income usually negotiated at an annual rate. Practitioners on salary are guaranteed a predetermined level of income as long as they remain employees of the group. Compensation represents the offered salary *plus* the dollar-value of any benefits added to the package. Benefits may include any of the following items: retirement plan contribution, medical insurance, malpractice insurance, disability insurance, life insurance, professional membership fees, costs of continuing education, vacation, and sick leave.

Drawing this distinction between salary and compensation may affect both recruitment and retention of practitioners. Consider this example: Suppose a group wants to hire a new associate. The group makes what it considers a reasonable offer of $70,000 annual salary but the practitioner hesitates and cites another competitive offer. Suppose further that the group now defined the offer as "total compensation" of $100,000 rather than salary. The figures might look something like this:

Base salary	$70,000
Group contribution, medical plan	$4,000
Life insurance	$500
Retirement contributions	$7,000
Vacation time ($200/day)	$2,800
Malpractice insurance	$15,000
Disability insurance	$700
Total Compensation	**$100,000**

Understanding the difference between total compensation and salary enables the group to help practitioners determine the amount of disposable income available to them on a monthly basis. This means that a dollar contributed in benefits and "perks" to the practitioner is a dollar not spent out of the base salary.

Income Distribution: Salary and Equal Distribution

Salary may be the simplest means of distributing income from an accounting perspective. Practitioners may enjoy the sense of security of knowing they will receive a fixed pay check on a regular basis. Salary is also a flexible means of distributing income—either compensation can be based entirely on salary or groups may prefer to mix a smaller base salary with some proportion of either a productivity or an incentive-based reimbursement structure.

Unfortunately, salaries are not easily linked to performance within the organization: A practitioner is guaranteed a certain income even if contributions to the practice are minimal (in terms of effective management or patient load). Income distribution by salary is strictly a group preference but practitioners should also look to connect performance by the group with total compensation.

Income is distributed equally when each practitioner shares the same proportion of net revenue. This is a good means of distribution in smaller practices when there is neither a sophisticated accounting system to distinguish patient load nor significantly different levels of patient care being seen by practitioners.

Equal distribution has some fundamental drawbacks. If the new group members have different equity stakes in the organization, there will undoubtedly be compensation issues. Whoever contributes the most to the practice will receive the greatest rewards. However, practitioners who contribute less equity to the practice but conduct a disproportionate share of the management responsibilities may also request an unequal distribution of revenue. Still another practitioner may request higher income distribution in return for his treatment and management of patients with higher severity of illness. Thus, among two previously solo practitioners, equal distribution is usually fair, simple, and equitable. Among larger practices or where there is inequity among ownership or responsibilities, this method is clearly flawed.

Productivity-Based Income

Productivity-based income provides a financial incentive to individual practitioners in a group by rewarding them for outstanding results as measured by some predetermined criteria. Measures of productivity may include:

- dollar production
- collected revenues
- revenue-to-expense ratio per practitioner
- patient visits or total encounters
- hours worked
- intensity of service
- gross revenue generated
- total net revenue per practitioner

Many practitioners enjoy productivity-based reimbursement because they believe it can be tied directly to individual performance. A practitioner can carefully select, or have selected for him or her, the performance measures desired by the group and concentrate his efforts. Unfortunately, this singular-minded attitude frequently develops at the expense of group goals. For example, hours worked is hardly an appropriate measure of productivity without some other measure of hours spent with patients, hours managing the business, etc. This leads to another point—measures of productivity should never be used in isolation. Multiple measures provide a means of checks and balances that ensure the individual and group incentives are aligned.

This last point is quite important and bears further illustration. Managers are frequently rewarded based on productivity measures. Suppose, for example, a particular manager is rewarded for gaining a certain market share for the product in his or her region. Perhaps the manager's productivity goal was 50% market share. At the end of the year, he or she returns showing management how he achieved a 55% market share. Unfortunately, the manager captured market share at the expense of revenue—cutting prices so much to encourage sales that even with high market share, revenue decreased. This simple example illustrates two points: First, again, productivity measures should never be evaluated singularly, and second, *management created this perverse incentive with a faulty system.* If you feel that productivity-based income is appropriate for your group, understand what incentives are created and ensure they are aligned with the group's goals and objectives.

Depending on how it is structured, productivity-based compensation may or may not be compatible with managed care payment mechanisms. For example, measuring practitioner total revenue in a capitated contract may not be appropriate since the group is compensated by fixed payments. This method of productivity, namely, seeing as many patients as possible, is incompatible with capitated payment (managing for only appropriate and necessary services). Perhaps a more appropriate measure might be to evaluate the recidivism rates for each practitioner's payments. To be fair, ensure this method is severity adjusted to avoid rewarding practitioners for seeing only the healthiest patients.

Productivity-based systems require some administrative work. Job descriptions should be formal, well conceived, and clearly understood by both the evaluator and the practitioner. Productivity measures must be tied directly to the job descriptions. If, for example, practitioners are expected to perform management responsibilities, the job description should appropriately describe those requirements, and performance measures should reward them for excellence in the performance of those duties.

Income distribution methods are perhaps most effective when used in some combination. The possibilities are endless and should reflect the ease of administration, financial feasibility, motivation, flexibility among practitioners, and an understanding of incentives created by the primary revenue source (fee for service, capitated, etc.) Besides the aforementioned, compensation could be based other elements such as:

- patient satisfaction
- cost control of overhead
- seniority
- value to the organization (possesses unique skills)
- contribution to the community
- quality of patient care
- research
- patient treatment outcomes

However you choose to compensate practitioners, the "litmus" test for validity may come at the end of the year. If a practitioner is highly compensated, beyond his peers, when the group practice itself is a struggling business, incentives may not be appropriately aligned.

Designing an Effective Incentive Program

Though no one incentive program exists for all practices, the following guidelines are as applicable for group practices as they are for large corporations. They represent a synthesis of tried criteria for effective incentive programs.

✔ *Simplicity.* Unless the practitioner can directly tie the incentive plan to his or her individual reward, the program will fail to reinforce positive performance. There is a simple test to check for simplicity. A practitioner should be able to calculate incentive pay anytime during the year (if any was earned). If the practitioner cannot easily do the task, the plan may be too cumbersome and may require revision.

✔ *Multiple Performance Criteria.* This concept was previously discussed in depth. It is disastrous in an incentive-based program for practitioners to become focused on one measure of performance. It will be done, intentionally or unintentionally, at the expense of other performance measures.

✔ *Consider Payout Provisions.* As you design any incentive program, ensure that the practitioner is seeing the reward in a timely enough manner to associate added compensation with accomplishment of specific performance criteria.

✔ *Maintain Internal Control of the Program.* Encourage periodic review of the program to ensure it accurately reflects changes. For example, did the group recently sign its first prepaid contract? If so, be sure to adjust the incentive system to account for the new business.

✔ *Participation.* Carefully balance individual and group goals in designing your system. Have you considered including nonclinical staff personnel in the design? If an administrative assistant performs duties that directly or indirectly affect successful outcomes, is this person adequately rewarded? If not, what message is being sent to the "team"?

Compensation plans should, above all, be flexible. As the market changes and the group adapts to changing requirements of payers and patients, the compensation system must also keep pace. It should meet a variety of group objectives to include some of the following: increased retention of practitioners, income security, increased and correctly aligned productivity, financial viability, equity among practitioners, profitability, and teamwork. An effective program keeps incentives correctly focused for practitioners and the group, and ultimately increases satisfaction. Compensation is a make or break issue in group development. If necessary, consult a qualified human resources or benefits consultant to construct a plan that is focused, flexible, appropriate, and effective.

SUMMARY

Factors that influence group behavior affect the interpersonal and group dynamics that occur as practices merge. Groups exhibit personalities and characteristics in the same manner as individuals. It is critical to understand differences in group behavior and plan for them. Understanding group dynamics is an important first step in assessing the fit between parties considering a merger. While all groups concede the relevance of developing solid financial and operational plans, failed mergers are often a result of parties with incompatible goals. By understanding the underlying forces that motivate groups and their behavior, practitioners develop a firm foundation for the integration of the two cultures. This will be critical as the practitioners enter the strategic planning and business planning processes.

As groups grow larger, individual status and roles become increasingly vague. This chapter illustrated how to identify individual motivations in a group practice. The change management task ahead lies in recognizing, acknowledging, and meeting individual needs in a growing practice. To this point, we have established common ground for the group practice and a common vision. We understand each other's personal ambitions for the practice—from both a clinical practice and a business perspective. The remaining chapters in the text are devoted to developing an organization that meets the group's collective needs.

4

Operations

T HE SUCCESSFUL PRACTICE *must be managed as an effi-*
cient clinical practice and business. Ideally, operational issues
should complement the clinical practice—not interfere with it. Move-
ment into new markets increasingly taxes practice operations. Reim-
bursement structures are varied, as are the informational requirements
of multiple payers. This chapter examines the critical business and
clinical functions of a group practice with emphasis on effectiveness and
efficiency.

IDENTIFY BUSINESS OPERATIONS

Most group practices are consumed by a desire among members to further advance their practice of behavioral health care, increase their income, and potentially reduce liability through a joint venture. With increased growth and increased complexity of mixed traditional and managed care contracting, group practices are a demanding environment to
effectively administer. Though one member may have an interest in undertaking administrative responsibilities, the other members must collec-
tively decide if such association is in the best interest of the practice. Areas that should be considered are covered below. Notice that these topics
are generally the same as what the solo practitioner or group practice manages on a daily basis. However, a brief discussion follows highlighting some
of the many issues that will need to be addressed.

- *Communications*—Group practices will be put at increased strain
  in interoffice communications, particularly if the group works in
  multiple offices. Consider installing a voice mail system to pass
  messages quickly and efficiently. Newest-generation computer
  software is also available to permit multiple users to work on docu-

ments at the same time. Conduct meetings to discuss business and clinical issues only as often as necessary and then not before a planned agenda is generated. Communications with local community and professional colleagues are also important. Particularly in a fee for service environment, your colleagues are an important source of referrals.

- *Consultation*—Before accepting a patient for consultation, consider first whether the practice is required only to consult, to consult and manage, or to consult and manage with the referring group practice or practitioner.

- *Coverage*—Determine as a group how you will cover patient loads on weekends, holidays, and days off. If each practitioner maintains an equal work load, the duties can be easily rotated among the group's members. However, if one practitioner maintains a disproportionate share of patients, this may put an unnecessary strain on the rest of the members. In this case, consider either adjusting compensation to reflect the added work load or hiring an associate.

- *Record Keeping*—A frequent source of conflict among group members is handling of records. Most practitioners are most comfortable with the system they previously worked with, but this may not necessarily be best for the group. Consider profiling other practices that have developed record systems that work well. Don't "reinvent the wheel." Some groups may consider performing outcomes measurement, which involves analyzing evidence to estimate outcomes, comparing benefits with harms (net benefit), comparing outcomes with costs (net value), and setting priorities based on available resources. This complex task will be made far easier if the group has a computerized records system.

- *Insurance Claims and Billing*—Claims processing has become increasingly complex in recent years. If you contract with an insurer or managed care organization that has an elaborate claims system and complete billing process, consider adding a small fee for this added inconvenience. Make sure all staff members know the correct procedures for each carrier, particularly if each contract operates under a different reimbursement scheme.

- *Purchasing, Receiving, and Inventory of Supplies*—This is typically not as complex an issue for psychological practices as for physicians. Nonetheless, the essentials for office management—copiers, computers, facsimiles, telephones—all require periodic maintenance and adjustment. Everyone should know the correct number for servicing the equipment, although clearly one staff member should bear responsibility for this task. Establish a budget for incidental office items and demand that the office manager "top off" the office supplies monthly.

- *Personnel Management/Secretarial Support*—As noted earlier, groups that cannot consolidate staffs lose the economies of scale and resulting decreased overhead of affiliation. These issues should be resolved before a merger is ever consummated. Afterwards, allow some flexibility for the office manager or practitioner-manager to hire additional support as needed (either full-time or temporary support).

- *Development of Group Policies*—Draft group policies early in the group's formation to allow time for practitioners to review and amend them and to grow accustomed to the new operating environment. Possible subject matter may include: vacation policy, retirement funding, call/coverage procedures, etc. Develop a standard procedure for clinical emergencies after normal operating hours.

- *Office Leasing/Maintenance/Other*—Ensure that the lease describes the premises your practice is renting, the guaranteed services (housekeeping?), and penalties for late payment. Will you rent furnishings? What are the group's liabilities in a fire? Have a competent attorney review the lease agreement. Look specifically for the following:

  - Is there a guarantee that the premises can be used for the purposes of practicing behavioral health care?
  - Is there a provision allowing the group to break the lease in an emergency?
  - Can the lease be terminated, without penalty, if the facilities no longer can accommodate the entire group?
  - Does the lease describe the renter's right to sublease any portion of the facilities?
  - Is there a stated limitation on rental increases? Is there a relief from inordinate real estate taxes?

Group members may chose to execute these functions as a group, with each member assigned certain responsibilities, and have one group mem-

TABLE 3   Operational Criteria for Developing a Group Practice

- Communications
- Patient registration and reception
- Scheduling
- Interpractice and intrapractice referrals
- Record keeping
- Patients' charges
- Insurance claim processing and billing
- Purchasing, receiving, and inventory of supplies
- Personnel management and secretarial support
- Data processing and analysis
- Computer network and MIS needs
- Community/public relations
- Insurance
- Purchasing and supplies
- Systems development and management
- Maintenance
- Credit and collections
- Statistical analysis and data collection
- Contract review
- Planning and reporting
- Internal and external legal requirements
- Facility design, upgrade, and maintenance
- Capital financing
- Liaison with third party agencies and government
- Personnel and staff management
- Salary and tax administration
- Development of group policies
- Call and coverage

ber coordinate activities. Or the practice may elect to hire a professional office manager. Office managers vary in experience, education, and business and leadership skills. It is important to establish up-front the relationship and spirit of partnership between the entity's members and the office manager. Regardless of who performs the function, this person will be key in executing office operations. A further listing of operational items to consider for the new practice appears in Table 3 to facilitate discussion and planning.

Two items specifically have considerable impact in group practices that differ from solo practices—management information systems and marketing—and for this reason, they are discussed separately. Your practice's ability to measure outcomes and profile practitioners may dictate the group's competitiveness for contracting with integrated systems. Management information systems assist providers in this and other processes. This information will be useful in the group's marketing efforts if marketing dollars are spent communicating to the right customer with a targeted message.

MANAGEMENT INFORMATION SYSTEMS

Management information systems (MIS) allow the group to manage an increasingly complex amount of information required for successful practice management. As the entity begins to negotiate contracts to pro-

vide care with local business entities and insurers, information, on treatment patterns for example, will give the group an advantage by providing
concrete, measurable summaries. Additionally, MIS allow management
and practitioners alike to conduct profiling to determine the outstanding
providers relative to their peers, as measured by multiple criteria. Finally,
management information systems are interactive and designed for rapid
recovery of information by various managers in the organization to permit
appropriate responses to information. They can assist in routine items like
daily billing and collecting, word processing, and more complex tasks like
assisting in outcomes measurement. Management information systems are
discussed at length in another Toolbox book on how to select a management information system.

MIS Reports

Typical systems report information in one of three general categories.
Listed in Table 4 are sample "standard" reports that vendors design to make
information retrieval easier. Most systems also have the capability to create custom-designed reports for specific information needs.

MIS Requirements

In selecting your management information system, consider the following:

✔ *Type of Business Entity (Structure).* Corporations, partnerships,
and other entities all have different business structures and therefore differing information requirements. Entities that have report-

TABLE 4   Standard Reports for Information Management

Contract Analysis, Clinical Analysis, Practitioner Profiling	Contract Compliance Information	Contract Data, Membership Information
• Executive Summaries	• Payment Audit Reports	• Requirement for Admission
• Activity by Cases	• Out of Compliance Notice	
• Performance by Contract		
• Performance by Service		
• Practitioner Profile by Contract		
• Simulations		

ing requirements to the state government offices may need a system to automate and download required information. As you select a legal entity, consult your tax advisor and determine information needs that may affect selection of an information system.

✔ *Treatment Services.* What type of services will be offered? Are services technology driven? Are they provided in an inpatient or outpatient setting? How will the system support these functions? These are questions best answered by the vendor for each system.

✔ *Risk/Non-Risk.* Risk-bearing relationships require strict monitoring of utilization patterns. Can the system track both capitated expenses and allocated expenses by individual provider? This ability to monitor clinicians for cost-effective care should be a key design consideration. The system should likewise be able to support the needs of non-risk-bearing relationships. Can the system analyze and identify outstanding group members, in terms of both clinical and financial performance?

✔ *Sophistication of the Payer.* What requirements for on-line information will the purchaser of the group's services have?

MIS *Planning*

Through information management, providers are able to distinguish their practice based on cost, outcomes, and other efficiencies. This holds in both a managed care and a non-managed care environment. Information also adds credibility to your marketing efforts by enabling the practice to document and communicate the operating efficiencies of the practice.

Information is at the very heart of market reform. Integrated delivery systems are increasingly looking to differentiate *their* services by benchmarking performance, generating "report cards," and profiling providers. To compete for and manage contracts with MCOs, your MIS system needs to also support these functions. Obviously, the dilemma involves assessing what is needed and whether it can be accommodated in the group practice's initial development.

Needs may also vary depending on the group's expectations of working under managed care contracts. When managed care penetration is relatively low (or practically nonexistent), a simpler, less costly system that provides general off-the-shelf financial management, word processing, and accounting may be sufficient. For any of these functions, most computer stores can provide a range of software and computer hardware accessories. Look to purchase software that can interface together, namely, spreadsheets that can be imported to word processing applications, financial software that can be downloaded to spreadsheets, etc. However, if your strategy involves significant managed care contracting, particularly risk contracting, a more sophisticated system will be needed. There is also a cultural changeover cost involved in converting from a simple to a more advanced system. If the practice office has become used to managing the practice with little MIS support, it may have difficulty adjusting to the heavy information needs of a managed care environment. As such, an assessment of training requirements must be factored into any purchasing or leasing decision.

Most current MIS systems can be tailored to meet a variety of needs. Careless purchasing, without an understanding of what the system should measure and report, can lead to a costly and an inappropriate system. What needs must the system satisfy? Criteria to consider in planning include some of the following:

- ✔ *What Is the Group's Approach to Market Changes?* Consider relationships, economics of contracts, restrictions on care, review of utilization, administrative costs, profitability, etc. In general, the group will need a more elaborate system to participate in third party contracting. This need is heightened if the group managed multiple contracting.

- ✔ *Present Information Needs (up to 6 months).* Conduct an assessment of the your current system of managing information. For the short term (when start up costs are high), is it adequate? Can you manage multiple contracts in the short term, should there be a need?

- ✔ *Future Information Needs (6 months to 3 years).* Will the organization participate in risk contracting? Will it add additional service areas not currently offered? What information will be needed to participate as providers for an integrated system? Are there future opportunities that will require MIS support? If needed, purchase a system that will grow with the practice through software upgrades.

- ✔ *What Can the Group Afford?* Can external sources provide accurate information? How much risk can be accepted in MIS technology? How long can the group afford to wait for technology changes? What upgrades to the system does the vendor support and how much will they cost? What can the group afford now? In the next one to three years? What is the timetable for implementation?

✔ *Confidentiality.* What are the system's capabilities to restrict access to records and protect patient confidentiality?

✔ *Information System Daily Operations.* How will the day-to-day use of the MIS be accomplished? What types of reports are needed? Who will have access to reports? Will everyone have access to the same data and reports?

✔ *Ability to Support Specific Informational Requirements.* What information is needed on a scheduled, routine basis (monthly, quarterly, semiannually) and what information is needed on an ad hoc basis? Identification of essential information now will help eliminate data overload problems.

MARKETING PLANNING

Developing a marketing strategy and plan can be as simple or as complex as the group desires. Understand, however, the difference between marketing and advertisement. Too many practitioners confuse a half-page advertisement in the yellow pages with a marketing plan—it is not, but it may be a component of a larger plan. Advertisement is a means of communicating to the market but, unfortunately, when advertising is used without a clearly defined market, dollars are carelessly spent without a means to measure success. This section is designed to assist you in developing a *strategy* that delivers a clearly articulated message to market segments that identify and communicate with your desired market, as defined by treatment preference or source of revenue or both. This subject is covered in the Toolbox book detailing how to market your practice.

Step 1—Determine the Group's Customers

Are patients your only customers? Who are your primary and secondary customers? Primary customers are those who are direct recipients of services. For providers operating in a managed care environment, commercial payers may be their primary customers and patients their secondary customers. How sophisticated are the group's customers? Do they require specific information to make purchasing decisions? Who makes the purchasing decisions?

In low managed care markets, private payers make decisions regarding their selection of providers. In managed markets, the purchaser of health care services is not always so clear—in some cases, it is insurers; in others, managed care organizations; and in some cases, large self-insured employers. In larger metropolitan markets, purchasers may be a diverse mix of all of these. In general, the practice's customers are those individuals or groups that it already services and those it wishes to serve.

Step 2—Consider Environmental Trends

In this analysis, you assess external forces that affect the practice's ability to market and deliver services to customers. Consider the changes discussed in chapter 1 and apply them to your local market. Are there government initiatives in your area that may affect market potential? What is the current status of state Medicaid waivers, antitrust provisions, etc.? Are there current demographic trends? Visit your state's office of mental health and substance abuse. Also, state psychological associations can provide invaluable information. What trends are occurring statewide that may affect demand for your services?

Step 3—Analyze the Competition

During this step, the practice seeks to understand its competitors and assess their capabilities. To effectively market the practice, you communicate your practice's competitive advantages relative to other behavioral health professionals. Who are they? What are their strengths and weaknesses? In what markets do they compete? Do they offer complementary services or competitive services? What are their qualifications (doctoral level, masters, other)? What is a competing practice's cost structure and quality of care? Are competitors willing to share risk? Does their cost structure allow for risk sharing? Are they aggressive in their marketing efforts? With what result? Answers to these questions will help focus on exactly who the competition is and what its probable courses of action will be as the market changes.

Step 4—Know Your Practice

An often overlooked step in marketing is to understand the practice's internal strengths and weaknesses. What do we do well and what do we do poorly? This is critical as you try to match customer needs with internal strengths.

Step 5—Define Your Market

The practice's market will depend on previous decisions regarding payer mix and practice styles. Will the group pursue managed care contracts? Markets can be defined by commercial payers or private payers for health services. Patients are always customers and deserve quality behavioral health care but they may not always be your target market. Ask yourself: Who holds the majority of the behavioral health dollars? Is this a market I want to and can serve? Your answer to these questions defines your target market. Understanding that customers are not always the payers of health care services is the first step in further defining your target market. With a fixed marketing budget, the practice must decide what market offers the best opportunity to bring covered lives to the relationship.

If your practice has a diverse mix of business, develop a separate marketing strategy for each segment since each segment probably has unique needs. For instance, if you currently service private payers (50% of your current business), will you seek to grow, sustain, or exit this particular target market? In defining your market, consider or readdress these questions:

- Who are our customers? Who are primary customers (payers of your services)? Who are secondary customers (recipients of your services)?
- Is the practice's mission consistent with the group's defined market? (If we consider managed care a market segment, are we willing to practice that style of behavioral health care and, eventually, accept risk for our services?)
- How large is our market? How is this measured?
- What are the market's service requirements (price sensitivity, quality, outcomes, etc.)?

Thus, in developing your practice's target market, first identify who is included in your *total* market. Who are all the customers that the practice serves? Then, group customers that have sufficiently differing requirements—this is referred to as "segmenting" your market. Finally, choose a market (or markets) on which the practice wishes to concentrate its efforts and resources. This is your target market.

At this point, you have identified target markets, assessed internal and competitor strengths and weaknesses, and understood external market forces. How does the practice transition from a marketing strategy to a marketing program? Work through the following checklist to create a formal document.

✔ **Set Objectives.** Ask yourselves, "Why are we doing this?" The key to any objective is that it is definable and measurable.
   For example, a group's objective may be to increase third party reimbursement revenue by 25% in the next two years.

✔ **Develop a Positioning Statement.** Though it may seem formal, positioning statements clearly articulate why you expect customers to choose your services over your competitors. Link the statement to the customer's perceptions and distinguish it from competitors.
   For example, one practice may want to distinguish itself from competitors by the use of outcomes measurement and treatment protocols.

✔ **Identify Your Market.** Is this market measurable and easily identifiable?
   For example, to grow third party reimbursement at 25%, one practice may target its efforts to a primary customer base from (MCO name) and (insurer) that respectively deliver 10,000 and 15,000 covered lives.

✔ **Use Various Sources of Data.** To help identify markets and their characteristics, consider a variety of sources:
   - *Consumers*—U.S. Bureau of Census, National Data Research Corporation, Public Library, County and State Health Offices
   - *Practitioners/Group Practices*—American Psychological Association, Medical Group Management Association, State Psychological Associations
   - *Hospitals*—American Hospital Association, American Health Care Association, State Health Planning Commissions
   - *Payers*—Group Health Association of America, Health Insurance Association of America, Employer Coalitions, State Insurance Commissioner's Office

✔ **Prepare the "Marketing Mix."** The four Ps of marketing including consideration of price, product, promotion, and place.

- Price—Will the group work off its fee schedule or the payer's? What reimbursement mechanisms will it accept? What is the range of acceptable prices for each reimbursement mechanism?
- Product—What services will the group deliver? Where are there cost advantages?
- Promotion—By what means will the group communicate to customers? Media? Print? Other?
- Place—Where will the group deliver services? Office? Hospital? Satellite? Combination of any two or three?

✔ **Consider Other Functional Requirements.** Are there additional MIS requirements to service these customers? How will serving these customers change our internal compensation structure? What additional internal costs will be borne if we successfully market our services?

✔ **Develop a Budget and Timeline.** How much will it take to market to this group? How much can we afford? When should we see results? How will we measure success?

This section serves as a brief guide to developing a marketing strategy, not an advertising mix. Without understanding who your customers are and what markets can be effectively reached, advertising dollars are likely to become seeds on a windy day—you'll never know when they are on target. A marketing strategy and plan, even an informal one, will result in a focused and meaningful blueprint for communicating your practice's strengths to the right customers.

CLINICAL OPERATIONS

Group practices must determine, as an organization, how they will integrate delivery of care internally within their own office and integrate externally into a larger mental health delivery system. Managed care organizations and other payers are becoming increasingly demanding of their practitioners and, as such, some standardization of treatment among practitioners may help define success in such an environment. Payers want to see comprehensive health care organizations that bring diverse providers together and standardize their delivery of care. They do not want a fragmented delivery system where patients are lost between providers and cost redundancies exist. In response, payers, employers, and insurance companies are becoming increasingly sophisticated in evaluating quality, medical necessity, and clinical performance. This section explores various treatment mechanisms that increase internal consistency:

1. Standardize, to the extent possible, the approach to the delivery of care (e.g., treatment planning).
2. Document the practice's approach to the direct delivery of care (e.g., protocols).
3. Measure results against standard intervention (outcomes measurement).
4. Define and promote an appropriate and flexible approach to the treatment continuum (e.g., case management).

It is important that the group practice understands how it will function clinically—that each member understands how, broadly speaking, other members practice behavioral health care. The group will tailor its clinical approach to meet the group's desired mode of practice and to reflect the level of third party interaction in treatment decisions. In today's environment, the practice administers treatment in different modalities and, depending on the terms of the contract, under differing reimbursement. Providers can expect to operate using either utilization review services, case management, or some treatment protocols in contracting. These terms are discussed below.

Utilization Review

Does the practice routinely meet the purchaser's utilization review criteria? If the practice is not using outside criteria, are internal criteria standardized and in writing? Utilization review programs are becoming less important as practitioners assume greater risk through capitation and use databases to guide treatment decisions. However, utilization review plays a large part in traditional indemnity plan cost control as a method to determine medical necessity. Medically necessary services are typically those that:

1. are essential for assessment and treatment of a disease, condition, or illness;
2. can be expected to improve the patient's condition or level of functioning;
3. are in keeping with national standards of mental health profes-

sional practices as defined by standard clinical references and valid empirical experience for efficacy of therapies; and

4.   are provided at the most cost-effective level of care.

Notice that medical necessity, in a UR perspective, requires the cost-efficient and appropriate application of care. In capitated contracting, the provider is financially at-risk for the quality and quantity of services provided. Since the group practice is paid a per member per month fee for all care required, the resulting incentive created effectively negates the necessity for utilization review.

Case Management

Utilization review seeks to manage the course of an episode of care. Case management's goal is to manage the entire spectrum of care from initial assessment to successful clinical outcome. Where utilization review strives to exclude payment for unnecessary care, case management looks to channel patients into appropriate levels of care at appropriate stages of their clinical treatment. As group practices deal with more at-risk managed care contracting, internal case management will take on critical importance.

Case management involves treatment management over a longer period also. What fee for services and utilization review are to episodic treatment, capitation and case management are to comprehensive treatment. Developing a case management program will assist all members of the group in the management of the practice. Case management plans may include the following:

- How will the practice structure its approach to treating this illness?
- What is the scope of services included in this treatment?
- What guidelines will the practice follow?
- By what mechanism will we manage severely acute illnesses?
- What controls will be put in place? What milestones signal progress and success in treating the condition?
- Who will treat inpatient and outpatient cases? What resources are available in the continuum to supplement or expedite treatment?
- Who is identified as having necessary skills for certain illnesses?

- How do we recruit practitioners that understand case management?

Treatment Planning

Treatment planning focuses on a clinician's treatment philosophy and theoretical orientation. Group practices must be careful in recruiting associates and other members who share a similar concept of planning a patient's course of treatment. How do group members manage patients? What protocols do different members follow? In what setting do they prefer to treat patients (inpatient, outpatient, partial hospitalization)? Assessing a clinician's philosophy for treatment planning is a major consideration in assessing the "fit" between the potential new associate and the group practice. A practitioner who is not accustomed to having ancillary support staff to assist with treatment can be converted over time only if a commitment to the conversion is made.

Quality Management

A quality management (QM) program, at the group practice level, has the objective of preventing and correcting quality problems. QM is the thread that ensures your case management and treatment planning are on-target and provides for effective clinical and financially sound outcomes. QM includes treatment protocols, outcomes measurement, and customer satisfaction with service delivery. The rest of this chapter focuses on outcome measurements.

Outcomes Measurement

Outcomes are the result of a process. In behavioral health, outcomes measurement is the process of determining the outcome of a particular treatment at a specific point in the treatment process. Outcomes allow the group practice to maximize its own resources, namely, identifying practices and practitioners that demonstrate measurable and successful outcomes. Use of outcomes measurement allows practitioners to risk-rate treatments or to adjust treatment for various psychosocial backgrounds across the continuum of care.

Outcomes measurement has gained increased prominence throughout the health care market. In the public policy arena, health care costs continued to increase sharply over the last two decades with no appreciable change in public health. Measurement of outcomes can help establish national norms. Purchasers increasingly require providers to demonstrate value for their health care dollars through the use of outcomes. Some go even further and require their use as validation of a continuous quality improvement process done in earnest. Outcomes directly measure the validity of steps in a treatment process and therefore are a natural fit for quality improvement efforts. Finally, specific clinical research helps practitioners determine treatment designs that capture both efficacy and effectiveness of care.

Why should a group practice consider the time and expense of outcomes measurement? There are clear advantages to their development and use:

- Outcomes demonstrate to patients and/or payers a commitment to value and quality of care.
- Purchasers want to know what they are paying for.
- Outcomes provide scientific evidence to support competitive pricing.
- Outcomes allow for management and evaluation of providers within the group.
- They allow evaluation of the treatment process.
- Outcomes measurement provides ability to monitor ongoing care—focuses on treatment *throughout* the process rather than *after* the process.
- It provides a marketing advantage, especially among third party payers, though this is an outcrop of quality-delivered care.

Before the group considers conducting outcomes research, assess the readiness and ability of the group to conduct a meaningful analysis. What is the business environment the group operates in? Do payers demand outcomes measurements? Is their use a competitive advantage or not required in the local market? Assess the group's ability to conduct a detailed collection and analysis of data. Is the group cooperative and teamwork oriented? Does the group possess sufficient computer technology to conduct data analysis (even manual entry of information) and some statistical analysis? Can the staff be trained to support developing outcomes? Is there a champion in the group that is willing to undertake this project?

Outcomes measurements will be a necessary prerequisite for development of critical pathways. Critical pathways are specific steps that define treatment for a specific diagnosis. Critical pathways are like "decision trees." As treatment progresses to the next step, decisions must be made and the critical pathway guides the practitioner as to his next course of action. Critical pathways also identify resources required for the next step, such as any necessary materials, staff support, etc. Providers operating under capitated contracts may consider using critical pathways to maximize resources, standardize decision making, and identify sources of treatment variances.

Data collection is critical to effective outcomes measurement. As you select an MIS to support the practice, the level of sophistication in supporting your outcomes measurement needs should be considered. In instances when the group performs services in an outpatient setting, for example, desktop systems are already available to provide outcomes measures. For groups that operate across the treatment continuum (inpatient, outpatient, residential treatment centers, home health, partial hospitalization), sophisticated systems provide a more interactive environment for the practitioner to assess outcomes at each phase of treatment.

Providers are becoming increasingly accountable for treatment outcomes. Sophisticated buyers of health care services frequently require "report cards" that assess the organization's performance benchmarked against some national standard data. This requirement for outcomes information is expected to become a prerequisite for contracting with MCOs. Outcomes measurement will also be instrumental in determining the best practitioners in your practice to conduct treatment of specific illnesses among certain groups.

SUMMARY

The preceding section, like many others in this book, is designed to guide you through important decisions to be made. In this case, the group decides how it will practice behavioral health care and ensures this decision is consistent with market demands. Payers want report cards that provide clinical measures of successful treatment. Some groups may choose not to let market conditions dictate their style of clinical practice—this is an individual decision that may be driven by considerations other than revenue alone. To be profitable, practice a style of behavioral health care that is personally satisfying but also desired by your target market. Whatever style you choose, understand that the clinical direction taken by the practice must match the desired style of its practitioners and, ultimately, the group's business goals.

This chapter discusses some of the operational considerations for developing a group practice. It is critical to develop operating systems within the office that support clinical operations. Systems must be designed to operate efficiently in an increasingly complex market—one where the practice may see revenue from many sources under differing reimbursement schemes. The next chapter discusses options for funding the new group practice, determining costs, and understanding reimbursement methodologies.

5

Financing Considerations and Financial Management

C APITALIZATION OF THE PRACTICE *is critical for long-term success: The all-too-familiar story of entrepreneurs not prepared to fund their business from the practice's inception and through the growth phase is well documented. Capital requirements must be an integral part of planning from the outset. The extent of financing available is largely determined by the organizational structure selected. A desire to expand the practice or preference for servicing a niche specialty in a defined market may dictate the interest of differing outside investors.*

In this chapter, several strategies are offered as possible financing options. A comprehensive review of financial management is given in another text in the Toolbox series on financing your practice. This chapter, however, takes a detailed look at determining your costs and understanding reimbursement methods.

DETERMINING OPERATING FUNDS

Before looking for outside sources of capital, the practitioner must understand exactly what capital needs are required. Operating funds should include short term (up to 1 year), mid-term (1-3 years), and long term (beyond 3 years) capital requirements. An operating plan should address how you expect to provide funding at each stage of development and where funds will be accessed. Financial statements, specifically income statements, balance sheets, and cash flow statements, should be developed by a reputable certified public accountant. The operating plan is part of the larger financial picture for the practice, which addresses:

- pro forma income statements (monthly for the first year, quarterly for years 2 and 3)
- pro forma balance sheets (semiannually first year, annually years 2 and 3)

- cash flow analysis
- break-even analysis (carefully consider impact of managed care, state reform, etc.)
- schedule of anticipated capital needs—when do you anticipate further injection of capital may be required?
- desired types and sources of financing

This subject of working with a CPA bears further discussion. Practitioners are encouraged to understand the relationship between their cash and noncash positions, as expressed in the group's financial statements. A reputable accountant is an invaluable part of your management team for he or she can not only prepare financial statements, but also assess the financial health of the organization. As the practice continues to grow, your accountant should be consulted early to ensure a financial position that supports new operations, acquisitions, or hirings.

Practice Development Tip: A reputable accountant is an invaluable part of your management team. He or she can prepare financial statements and also assess the financial health of the organization.

Investors, such as banks, venture capitalists, and others, are looking for a careful, well planned, thorough analysis of the requirements for financial success. As such, avoid "snowballing" analysis, which projects unrealistic market potential. Try to anticipate expenses that may develop and plan finances accordingly. Investors want a realistic financial picture, not a dream. The investor should enter the relationship well aware of potential capital needs and associated risks. At this point, it may be helpful to develop a line-item accounting for both start-up and projected annual costs for the first three years. A sample format is shown in Figure 2.

SOURCES OF CAPITAL

Most practices are too small to make a public offering to raise capital. Partnerships, for example, may not together have the capital assets required to sustain the growing practice through possible early "lean" times to fund necessary capital requirements (facilities leasing, staff, etc.) Practitioners frequently ask how much working capital they will need for start-

		Start	Year 1	Year2	Year 3
Revenue					
	Practitioner Revenue				
	Prepaid Revenues (PMPM)				
	Other				
	Total Revenue				
Administrative Expenses					
Salaries and	Practitioner 1				
Wages (Clinical)	Practitioner 2				
	Practitioner 3				
	Practitioner 4				
	Practitioner 5				
	Practitioner 6				
	Practitioner 7				
	Practitioner 8				
	Master's Level Clinician				
	Social Worker(s)				
	Retirement and Profit Sharing				
	Insurance (Life, Health, etc.)				
	Other Employee Benefits				
	FICA, Practitioners				
Salaries and	Member Administrator				
Wages (Staff)	Office Manager				
	Records Staff				
	Receptionist				
	Total Salaries				
	Total Benefits				
	Total Salaries and Benefits				
Other Expenses					
	Rent				
	Mortgage				
	Utilities				
	Maintenance				
	Office Supplies				
	Telephone				
	Postage				
	Fax Copier				
	General Insurance				
	Marketing Expenses				
	Business Travel & Conferences				
	Professional Organization Dues				
	Continuing Education				
	Professional Fees (Legal, Consulting, Tax, Accounting)				
	Contingencies				
	MIS (Hardware, Software)				
	Total Other Expenditures				
Total Revenue					
Total Contributions					
Total Expenditures					

FIGURE 2   Sample format: projected revenue and expenses.

up of the group practice. The answer is contingent on what assets are brought to the merger, the likelihood of maintaining a revenue stream from each practice, and the attractiveness of the group to outside third party payers. In short, if the group is marketing a radical treatment style to a new customer base, plan for higher capital requirements (perhaps up to one year). If revenues are predictable but start-up costs excessive (new MIS, larger offices, etc.), also expect a need for short-term capital. The sheet on the previous page will help you work through these issues.

Possible sources of capital include commercial banks, joint ventures, venture capitalists, "angels," and personal contacts.

Commercial banks provide diverse sources of financing, including:

- short term credit
- commercial loans
- accounts receivable and inventory loans
- mortgage loans

Joint ventures offer a viable means of raising capital, but they typically result in lost autonomy. The practice, in concert with a joint venture partner, will typically share:

- a portion of its valuable assets
- its autonomy to conduct its practice and contract without some scrutiny
- its freedom to always determine its clientele base

Venture capital firms are generally interested in equity investments in companies with extremely high growth potential and in entities that plan to go public at some time. Venture capital may be a viable option if your practice is experiencing unplanned growth and there is a resulting need for capital. Be aware though, as compensation for the risk of the practice, venture capitalists may demand a voice in company management and a seat on the board of directors.

Venture capitalists are a diverse group. Targeting the right listing of venture capital companies is an exercise in and of itself. Venture capital firms vary by geography, industry specialization, stage of company development, and size of investment preferences. They will typically require a comprehensive business plan to serve as a road map of the practice development, financing, operations, and management. Key ideas a venture capitalist may target in the business planning include the following:

- Is the management team for the practice able to grow the business rapidly and successfully?
- Is there a market-driven need for the services?
- Is market potential large enough?
- Do barriers to entry exist?
- How much capital will be required and how will it be utilized?
- What exit strategies are possible? How does the group get out of the business if it turns sour?
- Does the practice understand how to interface in a managed care environment?

A corporation (either S or regular) that desires to compensate retirement plans by offering stock options instead of cash can augment its company's financial position without consuming precious cash reserves. This serves as an incentive to employees through equity ownership of the newly founded company and protects liquid assets critical for early business development.

Practitioners wishing to contact or learn more about venture capital firms are encouraged to write to the National Venture Capital Association at the following address:

> National Venture Capital Association
> 1655 North Fort Myer Drive
> Suite 700
> Arlington, VA 22209

The following guides offer additional information on the topic:

- *Pratt's Guide to Venture Capital Sources*, edited by David Schutt and Yong Lim, Venture Economics Publishing, a division of SDC Publishing, Inc., 40 West 57th Street, Suite 802, New York, NY 10019.
- Technology Capital Network, MIT Enterprise Forum of Cambridge, Inc., 201 Vassar Street, Building W59-MIT, Cambridge, MA 02139.

Angels are wealthy individual investors who are former entrepreneurs or executives who invest in entrepreneurial companies. Many investment clubs across the country serve as a network to reach this group of investors. The National Venture Capital Association (NVCA) publishes a listing of these clubs.

Many first-time entrepreneurs underestimate the value of their *personal network* of friends and family. Do group practitioners have any personal contacts that have access to capital and might be willing to invest in the practice? Important points to consider include: (a) How much equity should be relinquished to these investors? (b) What will be their involvement in practice operations and decision making? (c) How will this business relationship affect personal relationships?

PRICING OF SERVICES

Although a full course in cost accounting and, particularly activity-based costing, is beyond the scope of this text, the principles are very important to understanding the group's costs for its services and, ultimately, for effectively pricing its services. This is especially critical in negotiating risk-sharing contracts where the practice and individual member liability are at financial risk. Marketing managers and financial personnel frequently make the mistake of pricing their services to cover cost plus some arbitrary percentage of margin. This fails to consider what the market will bear for certain services. This section is designed to *help you determine total cost for a specific procedure on a per patient basis*. This will help ensure that pricing considers the procedure's full (fixed and variable) costs.

Cost accounting can be performed in-house; however, in larger group practices with multiple revenue-producing internal practices, a qualified cost accountant may prove helpful. Regardless of which avenue you choose, allocation of cost for the purpose of assigning full costs for a patient visit is a critical exercise and should be performed with a general understanding of key principles.

If the group practice chooses to use a cost accountant, members should nonetheless involve themselves in understanding the allocation of costs. Cost accounting makes reasonable assumptions about where indirect costs (that is, costs common to the entire practice and not one practitioner or group) should be allocated, but only practitioners closest to the costs will be able to give the accountant specific instructions and clear guidance for a successful cost-based accounting engagement.

At this point, some definitions, as defined in Table 5, may be helpful.

TABLE 5   Definitions of Costs

Full Costs	Full costs are the sum of total fixed costs plus an allocated proportion of variable costs
Fixed Costs	Fixed costs are costs that never change regardless of the volume activity. Salaries and rent are common examples
Variable Costs	Variable costs change relative to the volume or level of activity involved. Utilities, especially electricity, are common variable costs. The more you use, the greater the cost

Cost accounting is a separate discipline in and of itself. However, to reduce this procedure to its simplest form, the following text illustrates the development of full costs for a hypothetical practice.

Note: The following example is quite technical in nature and, without a prior understand of cost accounting, may seem difficult to follow. The objective of the exercise is to illustrate the process of developing the costs for a group's services. Determining full costs is not only a function of the time involved in delivering counseling, but also a proportion of the overhead. This is what is meant by the term "allocation" of costs—we will allocate a proportion of the overhead to each service that delivers revenue to the practice. In this way, the group will know the true costs of delivering a service and, ultimately, can use this information in developing competitive pricing.

Group Practice Example: The Main Street Clinic is a partnership of seven behavioral health practitioners that provide the following services: adult/adolescent/child substance abuse (SA) services, marriage and family treatment, learning disorder services, anxiety disorders treatment, neuropsychological services, and psychological testing. The group is located in one facility with 3,000 square feet of office space. An office manager (salary $60,000) serves the group as well as a receptionist (salary $25,000), two clerks for office support and medical records (salary $25,000 each), and two psychology assistants (salary $30,000 each).

Step 1: Assign Responsibility Centers

In larger medical organizations, responsibility centers may include radiology, pathology, and orthopedics. They all share the same criteria, namely, that each is responsible for a health care activity and has decision-making authority. The leader of a responsible center typically has control over use of resources. Even in a small partnership, one practitioner can fit this definition of a responsibility center. Responsibility centers can be defined as an activity, a function, or a group or individual. They generally take a given set of resources (costs), perform a function (i.e., counseling), and generate an outcome (revenue). All responsibility centers are revenue or cost-generating entities.

In our example, responsibility centers could be classified as:

Contribution Centers	Cost Centers
Substance Abuse (3 doctoral providers)	*Administration (1 personnel)*
Marriage (1 doctoral provider)	*Reception (1 personnel)*
Learning (1 doctoral provider)	*Records (2 personnel)*
Neuropsychology (1 doctoral provider)	
Testing (1 doctoral provider)	

Table 6 summarizes sample financial and nonfinancial data for use in our example.

At this point, a decision must be made regarding the two psychology assistants. Are they a cost center or do they provide additional revenue? For this example, we will assume they work within the substance abuse part of the practice and, therefore, we include their salaries in this responsibility center.

TABLE 6   Summarized Sample Financial Data

	FFS Gross Charges	Direct Costs	Square Footage (sq ft/% total)	Personnel
Contribution Centers				
SA	$370,000	$290,000	1,000 / 20%	3
Marriage	175,000	110,000	500 / 10%	1
Learning	85,000	50,000	500 / 10%	1
Anxiety	100,000	85,000	250 / 5%	1
Neuro	125,000	70,000	500 / 10%	1
Testing	150,000	60,000	500 / 10%	1
Cost Centers				
Administration		93,000	500 / 10%	1
Reception		28,000	250 / 5%	1
Records		66,000	1,000 / 20%	2
Total	1,005,000	852,000	5,000 / 100%	12

Step 2: Trace Revenues and Costs to Responsibility Centers

In this step, assign gross charges for the contribution centers and direct costs for both the contribution and the cost centers. Be careful to include as direct costs only those items that are directly related costs to that specific center (not shared costs). Direct costs would include salaries, benefits, supplies, insurance, equipment (not shared equipment), etc. In columns 3 and 4 of Table 6, we include nonfinancial information that will form the basis of allocating costs.

Step 3: Allocate Costs

There is no absolute rule in defining a basis for allocating costs. The term "basis" refers to the medium used to assign the percentages of cost. In this example, since all departments share some amount of office space, we chose square footage as one measure to allocate costs. Another convenient basis to allocate costs is using the staff involved in each center.

Allocation involves taking all the associated direct costs of a cost center and assigning them in some meaningful proportion to the rest of the contribution and cost centers. In this case, we want to know how much of the costs of administration should be borne by the substance abuse center? How much reception costs should the marriage counselors bear?

Note that when costs are allocated, they are allocated to *all* centers. In this case, we chose to allocate administration first. Its costs are allocated, on the basis of personnel count, to reception ($8,370), records ($16,740), and all contribution centers ($8,370 each). It then is a closed cost center—there are no more administrative costs to allocate. We then allocate receptionist costs to records ($8,728) and the contribution centers. (At this point, their direct costs include their original direct costs plus those allocated from records.) This process is continued until all reception costs are allocated. Finally, the records costs are allocated to the five contribution centers, since there are no cost centers left to allocate to. When all costs are allocated, we apply an adjustment or allowance factor and add all costs. This sum is our full costs.

Let's examine this process step-by-step in our example:

First, decide the order of allocation and by what basis each cost will be allocated. In this case, we choose administration first. As a rule, select the cost center that provides the most overall benefit as the first to allocate costs.

Cost Center	Allocation Order	Basis
Administration	1	Personnel Count
Reception	2	Square Footage
Records	3	Personnel Count

Allocation of administrative costs on the basis of personnel count:

For SA: 3 personnel / 12 total - 1 administration = 27%
      .27 x $93,000 = $25,110 = admin. costs allocated to SA

For Marriage: 1 personnel / 12 total - 1 administration = 9%
9% x $93,000 = $8,370 = admin. costs allocated to Marriage

Learning:	$8,370
Anxiety:	$8,370
Neuro:	$8,370
Testing:	$8,370
Reception:	$8,370
Records	$16,740 (note: figures include some rounding error)

Notice costs of administration were allocated to all contribution centers and the other cost centers. Now, in the same manner, allocate costs of the receptionist on a square footage basis. However, the total receptionist cost to allocate is $28,000 direct costs plus $8,370 (the new costs we just allocated from administration), or $36,370 total.

For SA: 1,000 sq ft / (5,000 total - 500 administration -
        250 reception) = 24%
        .24 x $36,370 (total reception costs) = $8,728

Marriage:	$4,364
Learning:	$4,364
Anxiety:	$2,182
Neuro:	$4,364
Testing:	$4,364
Records:	$8,728 (note: figures include some rounding error)

Next, allocate records costs using patient visits for the allocation base. Remember to use the sum of records direct costs ($66,000) plus its allocation for *administration ($16,740) plus its allocation for reception ($8,728), or $91,468 total. The math looks like this:*

> *For SA: 3 personnel / (12 total - 1 administration - 1*
> *reception - 2 records) = 38%*
> *38% x $91,468 = $34,758*

Marriage:	$11,586
Learning:	$11,586
Anxiety:	$11,586
Neuro:	$11,586
Testing:	$11,586 (note: figures include some rounding error)

Finally, let's determine the cost of each procedure, as shown in Table 7.

TABLE 7   Sample Costs of Each Procedure

	SA	Marriage	Learning	Anxiety	Neuro	Testing
Direct costs	$290,000	$110,000	$50,000	$85,000	$70,000	$60,000
Allocations						
Administration	25,111	8,370	8,370	8,370	8,370	8,370
Reception	8,728	4,364	4,364	2,182	4,364	4,364
Records	34,758	11,586	11,586	11,586	11,586	11,586
Full cost	358,597	134,320	4,320	107,138	94,320	84,320
Patient visits	21,000	10,000	5,000	6,000	7,000	17,000
Full cost/visit	$17.08	$13.43	$14.86	$17.86	$13.47	$4.96

Cost accounting is rarely a fun exercise, and for this reason, many practitioners relinquish the burden to a qualified accountant. Unfortunately, those practitioners often do not let the same consultant develop *pricing* for their services and, as a result, pricing is done without a full knowledge of the cost to deliver the services. If you choose to have a consultant assist you with cost accounting, work with him or her to identify all sources of cost to the service. He or she cannot possibly know this without your input. In this way, you will have a clear picture of your cost structure and a solid basis for effectively pricing the group's services.

REIMBURSEMENT METHODS FOR CLINICAL PSYCHOLOGIST SERVICES

Fee for Service

A group practice should develop a set fee schedule through which all practitioners are reimbursed. Either contracting with a carrier will occur on the carrier's fee schedule, or it may accept your schedule, usually requiring some fixed percentage discount (i.e., Carrier X will contract for a 20% discount off the group's fee schedule). Here is the reason you must understand the costs of delivering services: Suppose a group pursues a contract whose carrier requires use of its fee schedule at a discount of 20%. If the group does not understand the internal costs of delivering the requested services, it is impossible to determine the financial impact of the offer. Similarly, if the group's fee schedule does not consider costs, it is similarly impossible to negotiate any discounts. When would you know where the service is priced at break-even (where price equals costs)?

Providers should receive the carrier's fee schedule up-front. Often, fee schedules are calculated on U&C, or usual and customary charges. This is based on large databases, which reflect the charges of other practitioners with similar experience delivering the same services. Usually, the fees are adjusted for regional overhead costs (malpractice premiums and cost of living). If such a schedule is provided, ask to see your relevant current procedural terminology codes before services are rendered. Challenge the validity of the schedule if fees seem unrealistic, particularly if you have a good understanding of the full costs for providing the services.

Capitation

Capitation is a form of reimbursement frequently used by third party payers. As described in chapter 1, capitation is a fixed payment paid per member per month for all services required. This means that the provider is responsible and receives payment whether the patient never uses the services, requires re-treatment for previously delivered services, or simply requires intensive behavioral health care. The group practice must understand two essential criteria for success in capitated contracts: What is the scope of services and what is the expected utilization?

Providers in all medical and behavioral health care disciplines must understand exactly the services they are required to deliver (and are getting reimbursed for). For example: If the contract specifies that the group will deliver outpatient services, ask exactly what outpatient services are covered. Family therapy? Group therapy? Testing? Do not sign any contract unless you understand the scope of the services.

Practice Development Tip: In capitated contracting, providers are at financial risk for the contracted services (referred to as "scope of services") and the utilization of those services. Actuarial modeling is essential to ensure the capitated premium reflects fair compensation for the financial risk of delivering the services.

If the list of services includes procedures you cannot perform in-house, the group must either negotiate this out of the contract or consider contracting for the service. Bear in mind, however, that once the group contracts for services, all referrals are paid entirely by the group practice though its capitated payment. Therefore, if this is an option, ask the carrier if referrals must be made to its list of providers. If so, is there one that reflects your practice style and has control over its costs?

What utilization assumptions has the carrier made in offering its capitated rate? How many patients per 1,000, a common measure, should the practice expect from the contract. What are the demographics of the group and has the price developed been adjusted for age and sex? These questions are critical in determining the frequency of expected services. Remember, in a capitated contract, the practice earns greater revenue when fewer patients use the services—in fact, the practice is paid whether or not services are required. Therefore, understand the expected utilization of the covered population. If the contract is substantial, consider hiring a qualified actuary to evaluate the proposed offering. Actuaries can model the expected effect on revenues and determine the appropriateness of any adjustments made by the carrier. Finally, the actuary can forecast expected revenue (or losses) under the proposed price and can recommend a more appropriate price as required.

Risk-sharing contracts can be quite satisfying and lucrative for the group practice, providing the scope of services and projected utilization are clear and appropriate. As with any fee schedule arrangement, check to see if there are annual adjustments to the rate to account for unexpectedly high utilization or inflation adjustments. The concepts of evaluating fee for service and capitated offerings, as well as negotiating for better rates, are discussed further in a text in this series covering contracting with managed care or contracting on a capitated basis.

Reimbursement Under Medicare

In order to become a Medicare provider, you must obtain a provider number from your local Medicare carrier. While the process will vary slightly among carriers, most require that you request an application form in writing. In most cases, the process takes about six weeks to complete.

How much to charge a Medicare client, how much Medicare reimburses, and how much psychologists may collect are questions often asked. The answers are not simple and become more difficult because psychologists are paid under two different methodologies for determining Medicare payment. In 1992 the Health Care Financing Administration (HCFA) initiated a new payment system known as the Resource-Based Relative Value Scale (RBRVS). Psychologists are paid under RVRBS only for their diagnostic services. Therapeutic services are reimbursed under the old fee-charge system.

Formal rules regarding payment to psychologists have yet to be issued. HCFA has instructed Medicare carriers to continue to reimburse "clinical psychologists" for therapy services as they were paid under interim instructions. This means that, for now, psychologists are paid under the old fee-charge system at the rate of 80 percent of participating psychiatrists' adjusted prevailing charges for therapy services. Each January there is an inflation update of about 3%. Diagnostic services are paid under the new RBRVS fee schedule at 100 percent of the physician rate.

Specific information regarding inpatient, outpatient reimbursement, excluded services, restrictions, and hospital setting is available from the APA Practice Directorate. You may request *Medicare Guidelines for Psychologists*, revised in August 1994, by contacting the Directorate.

Reimbursement Under Medicaid

Most Medicaid programs across the country provide coverage for a psychologist's services. However, in many areas, they also provide coverage for services provided by limited license psychologists. To determine the coverage available in your state, contact the Medicaid office for a copy of the state's mental health plan for specific information on coverage, payment, and reporting requirements.

Reimbursement Under Other Carriers

Payment for a psychologist's services is determined by the benefit coverage outlined by each subscriber's insurance policy. Based on the structure of the benefit package, payment can range from 70 to 80% of the prevailing reasonable charge for the specific geographic area. There may be limitations to the place of service, number of sessions covered, and some pre-authorization requirements. Each patient's benefit structure should be thoroughly evaluated prior to the initiation of treatment to avoid payment issues later.

SUMMARY

The first part of this chapter explores sources of capital for the new group practice as well as determining up-front costs. In the second half, we explore accessing costs for services and use this information in developing competitive pricing and evaluating third party reimbursement. Providers should consider hiring outside professionals to assist them in this process, especially for groups in their infancy. Your practice is a business, and mismanagement of its financial affairs in the early development can be particularly difficult to overcome. A qualified advisor can guide you through financial management and help ensure that contracts signed make good financial sense.

6

Governance

AN EFFECTIVE GOVERNANCE *structure has mechanisms and checks and balances to steer day-to-day decisions as well as more complex strategic and financial decisions. For example, a board of directors cannot become overwhelmed in daily operational activities of the entity, depriving the organization of its insight on broader, strategic issues. Similarly, administrators stay in touch with day-to-day operations as well as support strategic planning. Ideally, both entities operate cohesively, understanding their separate missions but further understanding the importance of their collective overlapping responsibilities for the health of the organization.*

This chapter focuses on governance structure issues that balance leadership and practice management. Not all groups need boards of directors or managers—the decision is driven by the entity structure selected and the members' propensity for practice management. However, basic decision-making issues remain the same regardless of the structure. Practitioners must consider the necessary governance issues to designing a practice structure that supports both clinical and business goals.

GOVERNANCE STRUCTURE ISSUES

A common mistake in forming groups is to confuse the issues of equity and governance. Equity refers to an individual's stake in the business—his or her degree of ownership—as reflected by shares of stock, percentage of revenues, etc. Governance refers to the governing, control, or management of the practice. The two are unrelated. For example, partners with equal ownership in the practice may not necessarily share equal governance. Perhaps one practitioner brought more to the relationship in terms of reputation or capital and, as compensation, requested a greater share in the management of the organization. This is independent of ownership of the practice. Equity positions in a practice are typically structured by the financial risk assumed by each member—governance should be structured according to the individuals most qualified to lead and govern the practice.

Theory suggests that successful organizations are structured less along ownership lines than they are by matching environmental dynamics with the correct skill sets. Research also suggests that financial performance is a function of successful governance in the form of a strong, visionary boards of directors, executive committees, and administrative management. Among these groups typically emerges an "inner circle" of management that effectively makes the organization work on a daily basis.

Table 8 depicts typical group structures—some with managers, board of directors, practitioner-managers, committee rule, and outside contractor management. Note that no single method is without flaws nor is one necessarily better than another. The decision in selecting a governance structure should reflect the practitioners' desire to involve themselves in day-to-day management of the group, their skills in successfully doing so, and their comfort in empowering themselves or others with management responsibilities.

Authority of Managers

Clearly articulating a manager's duties is critical toward effective practice management. The first difficult task will be deciding who will manage day-to-day operations. Again, what is the practitioners' vision of success? Absolute freedom to practice without administrative burdens? Some practitioners enjoy the administrative responsibilities of the practice—others do not. If this is the case, then hiring an outside manager may be a viable solution.

Select this manager carefully. Is there a shared attitude and vision of practice success? What is his or her experience in managed care and how does he or she see the practice integrating in managed behavioral health? The manager will be an integral part of the practice team — he or she will operationalize the vision and ultimately assist in off-loading routine daily operational tasks. The manager should also have a vision for the practice's success.

Other organizations may have a practitioner who prefers to conduct the administrative duties. The same questions are still relevant. How do the other practitioners respond to this manager-practitioner's dual role.

Will these duties interfere with the clinical synergy of the practice? How will this individual be compensated for his or her troubles? How are the duties and limits defined? How will the practice remove this person if the arrangement does not work out satisfactorily? This is a tenuous situation—more than one manager has felt abused by the tremendous (and in many cases, undercompensated) demands required to administer a successful practice. It can create feelings of resentment and distrust unless the members precisely define, in writing, both responsibilities and compensation.

The Board of Directors

One of the most difficult issues facing a group practice is its governance structure. Entities that fail to give governance proper consideration are frequently marred by indecision, unresponsiveness, or worse, inappropriate decision making. Table 8 gives some examples of frequently seen governance structures. There is no typical right or wrong—the effectiveness of a structure lies in its abilities to make difficult decisions.

Compensation is frequently an issue that tests the effectiveness of a governing body. Partnerships that develop a structure that gives everyone one vote frequently come to blows over this issue. In the past, it was convenient and appropriate in many cases to immediately distribute bonuses and salary increases as the practice continued to grow. It seemed a logical extension and reward for hard work and clinical excellence. However, many governance structures today have not transitioned to a prepaid frame of mind. In a risk-sharing environment, retained earnings are vitally important to protect the practice. Retained earnings may be required to invest in an equity relationship in partnering with an integrated system, for expenses related to merger and other growth opportunities, and for the occasional patient that requires intensive services in a capitated contract. Can the entity's governance structure break ranks with the past on salary and bonus issues to act in the best interest of the entity?

Structure, composition, and authority of the board of directors must be clearly established. Probably the single most important consideration should be the selection process. In multispecialty groups, all specialties should be represented on the board. Similarly, the groups should have a representative mix of different age groups. More than one associate fresh out of graduate school has felt ostracized from a board that represented only the interests of senior group members. The board should ideally be composed of members with diverse skills. For example, if clinicians all serve on the board, do any possess business and finance skills that may be required in deciding capital purchase issues? Does a board of key community business leaders properly understand the dynamics of managed care to make strategic decisions?

This issue of board representation deserves further discussion. Boards of directors often take on dynamics of their own. Group dynamics dictate that individuals will congregate toward members with the most knowledge of the subject or, in some cases, the most dominant personality. Guard against developing a board structure that permits one director to "bully" decision making. For example, if only one clinician sits on the board, would his vote count equally in decision making on clinical issues? Or would his vote count two or three times another member's vote on issues of treatment? Weighting each member's vote or weighting them on certain issues is a creative way of ensuring that specific expertise is accorded greater importance in decision making. Establish rules in the entity's bylaws to eliminate any possible prejudice or abuse of authority.

How much authority will the board receive? Boards that meet too frequently or have marathon meetings into the night are probably deciding daily operational issues rather than establishing policy and strategy. Give the group's CEO or administrator latitude to conduct daily operations and make responsive decisions. If further insight is required, the board may elect to establish an executive committee to partner with the administrator on key issues. Bylaws can establish how this committee is formed—it does not have to be permanent or composed of the same membership. Rules should be established, in writing, regarding the types of decisions the board and executive committee will become involved in.

Practice Development Tip: *As the behavioral health care market continues to change, directors' skills must also keep pace. These directors will make the financial and strategic decisions that will ultimately impact the group's success. Invest in their continued health care education to ensure that they understand market dynamics.*

In establishing the limits of authority for the board of directors, the entity's bylaws becomes an important document. Bylaws should establish operating procedures and voting majorities required for passage of board items. They should delineate procedures if all board members cannot be physically present for a vote. Bylaws should clearly address the authority and responsibilities of key officers (President of the Board, Vice Presidents, Secretaries). Some specific responsibilities that may be addressed are included in Table 8.

- ✔ *The board's authority to manage and control the affairs of the organization.* Be very careful in the language used in this section. If you want a board that does not have power to amend bylaws or articles of incorporation, then state this.
- ✔ *The board's authority to elect and remove officers of the corporation.* If the board is given this responsibility, is it required to consult with anyone else in the organization? How will voting occur—simple majority or supermajority? (Supermajority votes require some predetermined percentage over 51% to achieve consensus. A directive may pass, for example, if a supermajority of 75% of the votes are yes.)
- ✔ *Authority to issue shares of the corporation's stock, if applicable.*
- ✔ *Authority to borrow money in the entity's name in the form of promissory notes, debts of trust, mortgages, bonds, deeds of trust, pledges, and other securities.*
- ✔ *Ability to designate an executive committee for purposes deemed necessary by the board.* Again, details of appointing an executive committee should be fully outlined. Will the committee be temporary, or organized to deal with a specific issue, and then be disbanded? Will the committee members be appointed or voted on by the board or other body? Bylaws typically establish the executive committee's limits of authority.
- ✔ *Resignation procedures of a board member and criteria for voluntary termination of a board member.*

Almost as important as establishing the authority of the board is also delineating what activities it is *not* authorized to conduct. For example, boards are typically prohibited from implementing activities that also require shareholder approval, filling board vacancies, designating their compensation as directors, changing the number of board members, adaptation, or amendment of bylaws. Sample strategies for effective board administration are shown in Table 9.

TABLE 8 Advantages and Disadvantages of Governance Structures

Title	Description	Pros	Cons	Commentary
Single Manager (*practitioner*)	Manager is elected or volunteers; elected as an officer in corporations where bylaws outline responsibilities	Frees others for clinical duties; requires only one member learn administrative and management functions	Members may resent decisions or feel decisions do not reflect practice; manager may not have necessary skills	Risky unless duties are clearly outlined; may require lesser clinical load; special compensation may be appropriate
Single Manager (*hired manager*)	Manager is hired by the group members; duties are defined in either a job description or bylaws	Frees all practitioners for clinical duties, depending on the nature of the manager's responsibilities; can be screened to fill any required skill set currently missing from the practice	If duties are not made clear, actions may not reflect members' intentions for the practice; possible resentment among members that enjoy involvement in daily operations	Clearly delineate responsibilities, especially regarding contracting, planning, staffing, and capital purchasing. Decide up-front decisions that are the manager's sole responsibility
Management Committee or Board	A group of members is selected to manage the entity's affairs. Voting may occur through simple or supermajority	Diverse representation may appeal to young practitioners; allow others to abstain from governance activities	Senior members are typically overrepresented causing resentment; large boards create bureaucracies and slow decision making	If the group is a multi-specialty, ensure all disciplines are represented; avoid long meetings on small decisions
Democracy (*governance by all practitioners*)	All members participate in all decisions; members make decisions on regular basis or ad hoc as issues arise	Practice develops member base that becomes savvy to the administration of the practice; members take greater interest in affairs or practice; members participate in decision making	Inefficient; often gets bogged down in trivialities; forces involvement on practitioners who have no desire to become involved in daily activity	May be effective if structured to ensure only certain kinds of decisions require 100% participation. Still, bogs down in daily decisions. Could work if one member develops recommendations for the group to consider
Outside Contract Management	An outside organization is contracted to perform the most simple to the most complex tasks of practice management	Frees clinicians to practice mental health care; often these organizations come with significant experience and expertise in management procedures	Members may become too off-loaded and detach themselves from any management responsibilities; outside organization may not properly execute practice's vision for quality service	Works well if organization clearly understands members' vision for the practice; exact duties to be performed must be clearly defined; may want to start with smaller responsibilities until a relationship is formed

Bylaws

Bylaws articulate the entity's purposes and describe, in some detail, its board, committee structure, qualifications of board members, procedures for filling board vacancies, qualifications and selection of officers, indemnity rights of directors and officers, and amendments procedures to the bylaws. Bylaws are distinct for each entity and they also articulate, in a structured way, the degree of control sought by the founders.

The following is a sample format that may be used in constructing a set of bylaws for your organization. It may be helpful to consult other existing groups and read through their bylaws. Draw from other examples elements you would want to incorporate into your group's document.

Article One—Principal Office
- Name of the organization
- Location of the principal office

Article Two—Shareholder's Meetings
- Frequency, time, and place of annual meetings
- Who has the authority to call meetings
- How voting will occur at meetings
- What issues will routinely be discussed
- Procedure for calling special meetings of shareholders, board members, etc.
- Procedures for absentee voting
- Procedures for meeting adjournment
- Recording of the "minutes"

Article Three—The Board of Directors
- Nature of the board's duties
  - elect and remove officers
  - fix officers' compensation
  - issue corporate stock (if applicable)
  - borrow money
  - amend, repeal, alter bylaws
  - approve committees for fulfilling any of the above
- Number of board members
- Election of board members
- Procedures for filling a board vacancy
- Compensation of directors
- Resignation procedures

TABLE 9   Strategies for Effective Board Administration

Strategy	Considerations
Establish the board's stability	Are members prompt?
	Do they have necessary and relevant skills?
Promote continuity	Are terms of office sufficiently long enough to ensure understanding of relevant issues?
	Does voting for seats occur all at once or alternatively on succeeding years?
Strategically focused	Does the board meet too frequently?
	Are board members visionary and do they understand this aspect of the board's mission?
	Does the board use its influence in the business community to further the organization's market position, reputation, partnerships, etc.?
Educate the board	Does the entity prepare the board for new issues by scheduling continuing education, seminars, etc.?
	Do nonclinical board members work diligently to understand managed care dynamics? What does the organization do to promote board/administration unity?
Provide relevant information	Does the board receive information prior to meetings to allow members time to prepare questions?
Effective group meetings	Are meetings punctual and structured to ensure objectives are understood and accomplished?
	Is an agenda issued for each meeting (in advance)?
Allows for candid discussion and prompt decision making	Does the board allow all members to voice legitimate concerns?
	How is the board structured to ensure expeditious decision making?
Diverse mix of directors?	Are business, clinical, and community leaders represented appropriately?
	Are all specialties represented?
	Are differing clinical experience levels represented, as appropriate?

Article Four—Meetings of Directors
- Times/place of regular meetings
- Procedures for special meetings
- Method of notification of special meetings (to ensure all board members have the opportunity to be present)
- What majority must be present for the board to transact business (quorum)?
- Ability to adjourn meetings prior to a quorum (decision)
- Ability to act, in absence of a meeting, if all members agree in writing to act on a certain provision
- Committees', established by the board, adherence to the same provisions as the board

Article Five—Officers and Committees
- Delineates specific officers
  - Chairman or President

- Vice President(s)
- Secretary
- Treasurer
- Delineates responsibilities of each board member
- Indemnification of officers?
- Requirement for the organization to maintain liability insurance on behalf of its officers
- Procedures, rules, and composition of executive committee, if required

Article Six—Miscellaneous
- Procedures for inspection of corporate records
- Rights of shareholders
- Inspection of bylaws
- Others, as required

Article Seven—Amendments
- Rules for adopting amendments

Article Eight—Annual Report
- Requirement for an annual report
- Provisions for waiver of annual report (less than a certain number of shareholders?)

Article Nine—Transfer and Ownership of Shares
- Rules for ownership of shares
- Rules defining transfer of shares

Article Ten—Certificate of the Secretary
- Confirmation by the board's secretary of the legality and authenticity of the bylaws, in compliance with all applicable federal and state regulations

This sample outline covers the basic tenets contained in most bylaws. No one sample works for every organization and, therefore, you should tailor your bylaws to match the organization's requirements for responsiveness. Do not let the bylaws create an unnecessary bureaucracy rather, they should set reasonable limits and empower key directors and officers to make decisions in the best interests of the practice.

SUMMARY

Governance of a group practice has taken on even greater importance in this new era of mixed private and third party reimbursement. Decisions are increasingly complex, requiring skills and leadership in contract management, office management, negotiation, marketing, and strategic planning. Managers and governing boards can no longer just be astute business persons—they must understand the group's role in a changing mental health market. Market changes demand adjustment of internal operations, and leaders must be confident enough to make difficult decisions and manage the change carefully. Finally, governance of the organization must be responsive. Competition in many markets is fierce, and organizations that become bogged in administrative quagmires will miss open windows of opportunities that can quickly close. In short, effective governance must plan for control of the practice's business, manage internal and external changes, and respond to opportunities in a dynamic market.

7

Legal and Structural Considerations

L EGAL AND TAX *considerations are critical decisions but can be made only after practitioners determine their exact business objectives (salary, practice autonomy, etc.) Typical structured forms of a practice include: sole proprietorship, partnership (general, limited liability), limited liability company, regular corporation, and S corporation. Each of these organizations is discussed in detail in this chapter. As requirements for each organization can vary from state-to-state, consulting legal counsel competent in this area is imperative to successfully developing a group practice.*

This chapter discusses in general terms the issues surrounding selection of a legal entity. The remainder of the chapter discusses partnerships, limited liability companies, and corporations. Each topic is described, and advantages and disadvantages are highlighted. For benchmarking purposes, a sole proprietorship is also described since it is the business form probably most familiar to practitioners. Finally, the chapter considers antitrust issues.

FACTORS IN CHOOSING A LEGAL STRUCTURE

Choosing a business form is a critical decision involving many legal and tax considerations. Because each type of entity is treated somewhat differently, you should choose the one that most closely matches the group's business needs. Prior to selecting a business form, practitioners should consider the following items as discussed below:

- tax rates
- retained or paid-out earnings
- liability protection
- allocation of tax items
- existence of losses

- limitations on ownership
- financing needs
- potential for merger, acquisitions, integration into a delivery system of care
- likelihood of joint ventures
- compensation of owners/employees
- state tax treatment

Tax Rates. Certain personal services corporations, like health care, are not eligible for the graduated federal corporate rates and therefore pay the highest corporate rate of 35%. Clinicians should decide carefully how much they expect to earn in the first several years. In a sole proprietorship, individual tax liability can be up to 39.6% (up to 43% with a phase out of personal exemptions and itemized deductions). However, even with double taxation, a corporate structure may decrease overall tax liability on total individual taxation.

Retained or Paid-Out Earnings. A regular corporation does not incur tax liability for expenses retained for growth or other business reasons. The corporation will, however, be taxed on retained earnings. Retained earnings paid to employees, by regular corporations, as dividends are subject to taxation at both the corporate and the personal level.

Liability Protection. Consider the liability of the owners' personal assets. Sole proprietorship and partnerships generally incur unlimited personal liability in a lawsuit. Balance practice autonomy with the need to protect personal liability (although no organization protects practitioners from personal malpractice liability).

Allocation of Tax Items. Special allocations of tax items can assist the practice in attracting and rewarding highly qualified employees or attracting new equity capital to the business. This item is particularly available to partnerships and limited liability companies (LLCs), which are both discussed in this chapter.

Existence of Losses. If there are losses, LLCs or S corporations may be better choices due to their ability to pass losses through to the owners to offset other income.

Limitations on Ownership. S corporations cannot have more than 35 shareholders, while a partnership or LLC, taxed as a partnership, must have more than one owner (although an additional owner's status in the business could be as little as 1%).

Potential for Mergers/Acquisitions. In general:

- regular corporations generally can merge and reorganize tax-free
- partnerships or LLCs can merge with each other but cannot merge tax-free with corporations
  - partnerships and LLCs can generally be incorporated tax-free
- S corporations can merge tax-free

Likelihood of Joint Venture. Partnerships and LLCs allow for special allocation of income that may be attractive toward forming a joint venture.

Compensation of Owner-Employees. Health care plans and group life insurance are tax-free benefits to employees of regular corporations. Partnerships, LLC, and S corporation owners incur tax liability for this benefit. All organizations allow for options to permit employee equity in the organization.

Estate Planning Needs. Various business forms present different advantages and disadvantages for complex estate planning. In general, S corporations may be the preferred entity for complex estate planning.

State Tax Treatment. If your entity employs one or more staff members during any 20 week period, you will be responsible for:

1. unemployment compensation tax
2. worker's compensation insurance
3. contributions to a social security fund
4. withholding taxes and social security
5. compliance with state and local tax requirements

DESCRIPTION AND COMPARISON OF VARIOUS LEGAL ENTITY STRUCTURES

Sole Proprietorship

Sole proprietorships are the simplest forms of business operation. While there is only one owner of the business, this does not prohibit practicing with more than one practitioner. In most cases, additional clinicians are *contracted* for their services. However, ownership remains with the sole proprietor.

This single ownership brings with it both advantages and disadvantages as listed in Table 10. It is, without question, the simplest business entity to form and manage. The proprietor has sole discretion for all financial and operational issues of the practice. Business and personal income are the same so the owner reports all business income (or loss) and expenses on the individual's federal tax return. Taxable income is subject to both income and self-employment tax. Thus, the applicable Internal Revenue Service procedures are relatively simple compared with most other entities.

Other advantages also exist for the sole proprietor. Bookkeeping and legal formation costs are minimal. Since the proprietor has the discretion for all facets of the business, decision making is greatly simplified as well as other administrative bureaucracies. Sole proprietorship may be a less complex and less costly association through which psychologists can begin practicing together in anticipation of further integration into more complex entities.

With this increased autonomy come certain distinct disadvantages. As the sole owner, the proprietor assumes total liability for the practice. Often, creditors will require the would-be proprietor to pledge personal assets. This is somewhat balanced by the proprietor's absolute control and authority over all financial and operational phases of the business (and access to all the organization's profits). Also, most solo practitioners purchase general liability insurance, which protects their personal assets from catastrophic loss. The decision-making authority of a sole proprietorship may be a hindrance in complex decision making. For example, a decision to enter a risk-sharing managed care contract may be easier to make when multiple psychologists are financially tied to its successful or unsuccessful outcome. In a sole proprietorship, only the owner has financial liability for the risk of all practitioners.

Sole proprietorships may be a viable alternative for multiple clinicians

TABLE 10   Advantages and Disadvantages of Sole Proprietorships

Sole Proprietorship	
Advantages	Disadvantages
• Sole management responsibility • Most autonomy of any entity • Usually no legal entity required, some licensing • Flexibility • Sole decision making • Minimal cost of formation • Simple operationally and from a tax perspective • Does not prohibit practitioners from collaborating on a contractual basis	• Owner assumes all financial liability (personal assets may be at risk) • Other clinicians not vested to the practice • Fringe benefits to practice are not tax deductible • Sole management responsibility

who wish to practice together when one member wants sole ownership. Or it is conceivable for practices where one party cannot supply capital, such as a new graduate.

Partnerships

A partnership is an unincorporated business entity where two or more practitioners share profits and losses in the venture. Table 11 identifies the possible advantages and disadvantages of forming a partnership. A key feature of the partnership is the term "agency," that is, one partner is an "agent" of the other. This means that each practitioner is bound by the performance (or negligence) of another practitioner just as if he was performing the action. Termination of the partnership may occur by their own determination or death. A tax identification number is required, though no grant/charter is necessarily provided by a state. The partnership must file a federal and possibly a state return as well.

Partnerships are not subject to corporate taxation. Partners report income on their personal income taxes and are therefore taxed at the personal rate. Each is taxable only on his share in the partnership's profits. Thus, if one partner is a 70% owner, and one a 30% owner, profits, for tax reporting purposes, would also be split, 70-30%. Similar rules apply for state taxation.

Partners typically contractually bind themselves to the practice to prevent any possible misunderstandings. Items to consider include breakdown of profit-sharing, governance/voting rights in decision making, and

TABLE 11   Advantages and Disadvantages of Forming a Partnership

Partnership	
Advantages	Disadvantages
• Flexibility in governance, operation, reporting of income/losses • Professional collaboration • Partners maintain economically vested interest in the practice • Relatively simple governance, tax reporting • Flexible in dividing income, expenses, patients, profits, losses, etc. • Ability to incorporate many diverse practitioner interests in one single entity • Shared operating costs and financial risk	• Partners (GPs) have unlimited economic liability; LPs have little governing authority • No continuity of existence—may dissolve at the termination of a single partner • Shared authority can create decision-making conflicts

provisions for separation (either through retirement, disability, death, conflict, or voluntary termination).

Partnerships are generally classified as general or limited partnerships as discussed below:

General Partnership

A general partnership is an organization whose partners pursue the venture for joint profit. Usually a written agreement is most common but not absolutely necessary. Written agreements prevent future misunderstandings and thus are highly recommended. General partnerships must register with the appropriate state and obtain any necessary licenses. General partners (GPs) assume full personal financial liability for the partnership's operations. In addition to personal assets, capital contributions and partnership assets are also at risk.

Limited Liability Partnership

Limited liability partnerships are organizations with one or more general partners and one or more limited partners (LP). The essential difference between the GP and the LP is the extent of liability. Limited partners are financially liable only to the partners' activities for the cash and property they contribute and recent distribution. Conversely, general partners assume full financial liability including personal liability. Typically, however, general partners maintain sole responsibility for management functions; limited partners are simply investors in the organization.

Characteristics of a Partnership

- *Liability of General Partners*—General partners are fully at risk for all business debts, and both business and personal assets may be at risk to satisfy debts of the partnership. Most practitioners are advised to protect personal liability with general liability insurance.
- *Flexible Eligibility Rules*—There are no eligibility restrictions for partnerships (unlike S corporations.)
- *Advantageous Tax Positioning*—Partnership agreements can be constructed to ensure the entity never meets the criteria necessary to be classified as a corporation. Corporations are disadvantaged in that there exists a "double taxation"—on corporate income and personal income. This is discussed in greater detail later.

- *Special Allocations*—Partners may distribute income, losses, credits, or gains in any manner defined as "reasonable" to the IRS rather than based on ownership percentages (like corporations). Year-ends, for tax purposes, are flexible and may be defined to affect the profits or losses of individual partner tax liability.
- Passive Activity Loss—If a partner does not significantly participate in the partnership, then the partner's losses may be considered "passive" and not deducted. To meet the material participation standard, a partner must be involved in the business on a regular, continuous, and substantial basis. The IRS assumes all limited partners do not participate in a substantial manner unless the limited partner spends more than 500 hours per year on partnership activities.
- *Basis in Partnership Debt*—A partner's tax basis in a partnership determines his/her ability to deduct partnership losses.
- *Employment Taxes*—GPs are subject to self-employment tax on income; LPs pay this tax only on "guaranteed payments" from the partnership.
- *Alternative Minimum Tax*—Partnerships are subject to this tax only for research and developmental costs.
- *Estate Planning*—Partnerships are frequently used as vehicles to transfer an estate to other family members because there are no partnership ownership restrictions. Thus, in planning to transfer your estate to your heirs, partnership interests are more easily transferable than property.
- *State Tax Treatment*—Generally state taxes are treated the same as federal taxation.
- *Incorporation of a Partnership*—Usually, partnerships can fairly easily be converted to corporate form; however, taxable gain may result.

Partnerships are excellent vehicles in the following circumstances:

1. Personal liability of each member is not a concern.
2. Simplification of administration and operations is desired.
3. Professional collaboration is desired, especially in developing a contiguous group practice.
4. Business profits are distributed to partners.
5. Special allocation of profits/losses and other tax items is desirable.

Limited Liability Companies

Limited liability companies are among the fastest growing legal entities. LLCs are all similar to corporations in that they protect individual owners from personal liability. Only business-related assets remain at risk. States require LLCs to file articles of organization, and as such, LLCs are treated as separate legal entities. Typically states impose a fee upon LLC members that ranges from $50 to $10,000 annually.

The major advantage of the LLC is its exemption from federal corporate tax. Coupled with decreased personal liability of its members, the LLC is seeing huge growth. As such, LLCs combine two of the most attractive elements of the partnership and corporation. Table 12 further illustrates the advantages and disadvantages of LLCs.

Characteristics

- *Limited Liability*—As this is perhaps the major advantage to the LLC, proper legal formation and registration with the appropriate state agency is critical. Competent legal counsel is necessary to ensure regulatory compliance and minimize liability exposure
- *Eligibility Rules*—Generally, there are no eligibility rules except that there must be at least two or more members to gain partnership tax treatment.
- *State Tax Treatment*—LLC members (not the LLCs themselves) are subject to state tax liability. States typically follow the federal government's lead in classifying LLCs as partnerships when they meet the necessary criteria. Ensuring your entity conforms to state

TABLE 12   Advantages and Disadvantages of Limited Liability Companies

Limited Liability Companies	
Advantages	Disadvantages
• No double tax on distributed income (like regular corporations) • Limited liability • Unlimited number and types of members	• Relatively new entity—requirements vary from state to state • Tax planning for individual LLC members may be more difficult because the IRS does not recognize general and limited partners • Operating an LLC across state boundary lines may be more cumbersome • Creditors may be somewhat unfamiliar with the concept (though this is changing)

and federal guidelines for LLCs will be a critical process and one that requires periodic evaluation.

- *Special Allocations*—Like partnerships, LLCs offer the ability to structure income, gains, losses, deduction, and credits, within IRS guidelines, to benefit individual member's tax circumstances.
- *Certainty of Tax Status*—LLCs must be careful to ensure that they avoid meeting the criteria of a corporation or risk losing the single-tax advantages of partnership.
- *Entity Level Debt*—An entity member receives basis equal to the amount of contributed property minus the entity's liabilities. Basis measures whether later distributions by the business will be taxed. If the LLC meets partnership criteria, members may deduct business losses against basis, thereby impacting their tax reporting.
- *Passive Activity Losses* —LLC members are likely to be treated as limited partners in this area.
- *Alternative Minimum Tax*—Unlike a corporation, the LLC is not burdened with the alternative minimum tax (AMT), adjusted current earnings adjustment, or environmental tax.
- *Tax Year*—LLCs must define their tax year the same way as the majority of its members. For group practices, this will typically be a calendar year.
- *Benefits*—Items such as medical and life insurance, usually considered nontaxable benefits, may be taxable to LLC members.
- *Employment Taxes*—Generally, active LLC members that bear responsibilities for running the LLC are considered general partners and are therefore subject to self-employment tax. Nonactive members fall under the same rules as limited partners.
- *Penalty Taxes and Unreasonable Compensation*—LLCs are not subject to the accumulated earnings or personal holding company taxes.
- *Merging Incorporation*—Generally, LLCs can merge with either another LLC or a partnership tax-free. Merging with a corporation will subject the LLC to tax liability. LLCs can also incorporate tax-free.

The limited liability company is a relatively new concept but is gaining widespread acceptance nationwide. Currently, only Hawaii, Massachusetts, and Vermont do not recognize them as legal entities. While the

LLC combines the best features of both the partnership and the corporation, practitioners are cautioned to seek tax consultation as the IRS continues to issue rulings and judgments on this novel entity.

Regular Corporations

Most larger businesses are classified as regular corporations. Corporations are independent legal entities separate from their owners. They may be structured as for-profit, not-for-profit, personnel holding companies, or Subchapter S corporations. Limited liability and double taxation on corporate earnings are the hallmarks of this organization.

Among the legal entities discussed, the regular corporation is the most formal and requires special consideration (and expense) to maintain its unique status. However, for those practitioners with a vision that is captured in the corporate structure, the entity offers unique advantages. Table 13 illustrates the advantages and disadvantages of regular corporations.

Administration

The formal structure of the regular corporation is reflected by each state's requirements. Articles of incorporation (association) must be formed and the document must be filed with the state. Capitalization must be scrutinized to ensure IRS requirements. For example, if more than 50% of shares in the corporation are held by five or fewer practitioners, the practice will be considered a personal holding company (which has different tax implications). Again, a qualified tax consultant will guide you through the formal intricacies.

The management structure of a corporation is more complex than the

TABLE 13　Advantages and Disadvantages of Regular Corporations

Regular Corporations	
Advantages	Disadvantages
• Limited liability • Flexibility to raise capital • Employee stock ownership participation • Unlimited number of owners/types of owners • Highly structured management	• Potential for double taxation • Highly structured management restricts entrepreneurial environment • Costly to establish (licensure, consulting, legal) • Personal holdings cap tax at 39.6%

other entities discussed earlier. Corporations are required to have a board of directors and corporate officers that regularly meet and keep careful account of the business discussed. The corporation must maintain its own bank account, and books and records must be meticulously maintained. Although regular corporations enjoy benefits not afforded all other entities, they are subjected to more intense IRS and state scrutiny to ensure that they are fulfilling the legal requirements of corporations.

Taxation of Regular Corporations

Corporations are distinct legal entities and are taxed at a corporate level by filing a separate corporate return at the federal and state level. Practitioners, as both owners and employees of the corporation, are taxed at the personal level on their salaries. Although dividends at the corporate level are taxed at a much lower corporate tax rate, their issue to owners is still subject to double taxation. Shareholders must report this income on personal tax returns. This is the "double tax" that is most often cited as a corporation's biggest disadvantage. However, "reasonable salaries" paid to practitioners are not taxed at the corporate level but can be deducted as a business expense. Retained earnings are taxed only at the corporate level but not at the individual shareholder level. Shareholders are subject to taxation if earnings are distributed or if corporate assets are sold.

Characteristics of Corporations

- *Limited Liability*—Shareholders liability is limited only to the shareholder's investment in the corporate stock.
- *Corporate Tax Rates*—Corporate earnings are subject to federal and state taxation while dividends are subject to taxation in the shareholder's personal tax declaration (double tax). As discussed above, the corporation can avoid double tax effects by paying practitioners as employees and deducting payments as an expense. Though double taxation is a major issue, careful tax planning with a qualified professional can minimize its effects.
- *Eligibility Rules*—Corporations can have an unlimited number of shareholders, which may be a major advantage if the organization needs to raise capital in a public offering. The corporation has the flexibility to issue different classes of stock, appealing to investors with specific security or income distribution needs.

- *Flexibility/Transferability*—Flexibility in ownership is a major corporation advantage. Publicly traded companies appeal to both large and small investors as each is assured of a public avenue through which shares can be bought and sold. Additionally, publicly traded companies have required financial disclosures, which allow potential investors to readily evaluate performance before investment.
- *Ability to Finance Growth*—Corporations can raise capital through issuance of additional shares to new/existing owners, public offerings to attract additional capital, merger with another business, or issuance of stock as an incentive for current practitioners or for value in recruiting.
- *Tax Year*—Corporations can vary the fiscal year as different from the tax year of its shareholders.
- *Benefits*—Many benefits from corporations to employees are tax deductible at the corporate level and are nontaxable benefits to employees.
- *Employment Taxes*—Unlike partnerships and LLCs, employees and shareholders in corporations are not subject to self-employment taxes.
- *Stock Options*—Equity options are a powerful advantage in recruiting, retaining, and motivating quality practitioners.
- *State Tax*—If the corporation acts within multiple states (and a determination is made that the corporation owes state taxes), the corporation must determine which state's tax will be levied on which portion of income. This may be a key consideration in corporations that conduct business in multiple states.

S Corporations

S corporations have some distinctions not found in a regular corporation. This text will highlight only those important differences between the two entities.

The fundamental difference between S corporations and regular corporations is that the S corporation does not pay taxes as a corporate entity. Income is passed through to shareholders who then pay personal taxes on their individual returns. In almost all other forms it is identical to a regular corporation. It continues to offer limited liability and must meet most of the legal requirements of a corporation's structure and licensing.

Another key difference is that an S corporation is restricted to only 35 shareholders. This severely negates the ability of S corporations to raise public funding and offer employee stock options. If the organization does not have overwhelming capital requirements, this may not present a problem but it could, at some time, limit growth and force organizations to reorganize as a regular corporation. Again, this will depend greatly on the founders' vision for the practice. Will it serve only local markets or will future expansion require additional capital? Will practitioners be lured through equity options or salary promises? How does each state recognize the special pass-through element of the S corporation?

S corporations can issue only one class of stock. This may restrict the entity's ability to meet a particular capitalist's needs regarding ownership and security of investment. Therefore, all shareholders share the same rights to distribution and liquidation of assets.

S Corporations Versus LLCs

Generally, LLCs offer the same benefits as S corporations without the corporate restrictions. However, S corporations offer some advantages, particularly over regular corporations, under certain scenarios:

1. Regular corporations desiring to move into the single tax realm may consider the S corporation as a viable alternative.
2. If the regular corporation is operating at a loss, shareholders may use these losses to shelter other income. This may be particularly appealing to a new practice that expects to operate at a loss its first year or two until contracts, reputation, and clientele are established.
3. S corporations distribute all their income to shareholders and may be most appropriate for organizations that do not, or cannot, reinvest earnings due to accumulated earnings taxation.
4. S corporations can pass through the losses expected and incurred in a leveraged buyout to shareholders to help them offset other income.

When to Convert From S to Regular Corporation

As mentioned above, S corporations single-tax shareholders at the personal tax rate while regular corporations are taxed twice—once on dividends at the corporate level and once on personal income at the personal level. However, certain high income individuals may have personal tax rates that greatly exceed the combined double taxation of a regular corporation (especially if the regular corporation does not expect to distribute excessive dividends). A qualified tax consultant can assist you in modeling potential tax liabilities.

Professional Corporations

Professional corporations (PCs) are so similar to regular corporations that this text will highlight only differences. Generally, PCs are organized by health care professionals, lawyers, accountants, and other professionals that have a special and confidential relationship with their clients and customers. Some states do not recognize any differences between the professional and regular corporations, while others have slight variations. Consult legal counsel competent to explain differences in your state.

Some states limit malpractice liability of a shareholder only to tortious (acts done in committing a tort) activities either personally engaged in or those done by others under the shareholder's direct supervision. The special and confidential nature of relationships in this organization result in this malpractice compromise between the unlimited liability of a partnership and the restricted liability of a regular corporation. A disadvantage to this restricted liability is the usually high cost of malpractice insurance, which must cover both the corporation and the individual.

Officers and boards of directors in professional corporations are frequently indemnified by the actions of the corporation. This occurs in some states and allows board members and officers to participate in the affairs of the organization without the risk of litigation or excessive cost of liability insurance. This provision also varies from state to state. Some states do not allow multidisciplinary group members to incorporate as a professional corporation.

A matrix of the principal legal entity forms is summarized in Table 14.

ANTITRUST ISSUES

Introduction

Integration and mergers of practices in and of themselves do not violate the spirit of the antitrust laws. In fact, such organizations are actually pro-business in that market forces are at work driving cost reduction, com-

TABLE 14 Summary of Legal Entities

	Partnership	LLC	Regular Corporation	S Corporation
Liability	Unlimited for general partners	Limited to amounts invested and loaned	Limited to amounts invested and loaned	Limited to amounts invested and loaned
Pass-through of profits and losses	Yes	Yes	No	Yes
Limitation on entity losses deductible by owners	Net investment plus net income plus share of debt	Net investment plus net income plus share of debt	Nondeductible	Net investment plus net income plus loans to corporation
Subject to passive activity rules	Yes	Yes	Generally not	Yes
Tax rates	Income taxed to owners at marginal tax rates	Income taxed to owners at marginal tax rates	15% on first $25,000 increasing to 34% over $75,000, 35% over $10 million	Incomes taxed to owners at marginal tax rates
Special allocations	Possible, if substantial economic effect	Possible, if substantial economic effect	No	No
Fiscal year	May end up to 3 months earlier than year-end of principal partners	May end up to 3 months earlier than year-end of principal partners	New corporations: Any fiscal year. Existing corporations: Fiscal year with business purpose; automatic change permitted in certain circumstances	May end up to 3 months earlier than year-end of principal stockholders
Tax-free fringe benefits	Limited	Limited	All permitted by law	Limited
Public offering	Yes, some difficulty	Very difficult	Yes	Yes
Tax-free merger with corporation	No, but tax-free incorporation available	No, but tax-free incorporation available	Yes	Yes
Accumulated earnings tax	No	No	Yes	No
Personal holding company tax	No	No	Yes	No

petitive pricing, and consumer choice. Antitrust issues settled in courts regarding provider-driven practices rely most heavily on the answers to the following questions:

1. What is the degree of integration?
2. What is the market power of the venture?
3. Does the arrangement significantly foreclose development of competing groups?
4. Does the implemented contract unduly restrict competition within or outside the venture?

In the development of a mental and behavioral health group, specific care should be taken to avoid three specific illegalities, including price fixing, division of markets, and group boycotts.

Typically, mergers and acquisitions of practices enjoy a greater degree of antitrust flexibility than other entities. This is because antitrust allegations involve a conspiracy on the part of competing providers to perform illegal actions of price fixing, group boycott, etc. Once the merger is consummated, the two parties are no longer competitors and are incapable of conspiring with one another; therefore, the threat of conspiracy is diminished. This does not mean that mergers are beyond legal challenge. Certainly, conspiracy allegations can emerge in large markets between practitioner groups but the likelihood is reduced. Mergers must be careful how they conduct pricing when market share is high. High market share does not generate antitrust concerns unless the entity uses this position to conduct illegal pricing activities like predatory pricing (pricing below costs to drive competitors out of the market) or price fixing.

Introduction of risk sharing usually lowers the risk of anticompetitive complaints. When providers accept capitated payments for their services, their activities are at financial risk for profit and loss. If your group has antitrust concerns, accepting capitated contracts may be an alternative to lessen the scrutiny. However, providers are cautioned to carefully consider the capitated payments and are advised to seek outside consulting assistance before accepting risk-sharing payments.

Providers who wish to affiliate but cannot accept risk-sharing contracts may raise price-fixing concerns. However, a loosely affiliated arrangement may be done if each group, individually, is free to sign or reject the terms of a contract without undue pressure or fear of retaliatory pricing. Without such a stipulation, group boycotting, described below, becomes a major threat.

Description of Antitrust Terms

Price Fixing

Price fixing occurs when two or more distinct organizations share information and collaborate in setting prices, thus influencing market dynamics and compromising fair market competition. Two or more organizations that become truly integrated into a single organization are usually not at risk for price fixing.

- The parties must sufficiently demonstrate that the relationship is more a "joint venture" than a disguised entity to conduct illegal price fixing.
- Critical criteria to determine integration among providers—is there risk sharing among the parties?
- Demonstrated means of risk sharing—integrated claims administration, billing and collection, or significant contribution of capital by participants.
- Possible solution—merge the hospital and foundation under a common parent organization. Without monopoly power, such a single entity can lawfully set prices and exclusively deal or group boycott. All subsidiaries must work for a common single parent's benefit.

Practice Development Tip: *In selecting legal advice for your practice, look for a full service firm that is big enough to guide you through all phases of group development (to include business development, contracting, and state regulatory issues).*

Exclusive Dealing

The issue here is whether the entity prevents other players from the market, either by allowing practitioners to contract with only one group or denying a competing hospital or health plan access to a needed practitioner base. To determine exclusivity, a qualified consultant should:

- Define the relative services offered.

- Determine the relevant geographic market based upon penetration of the specialized service involved.
- Calculate total market share and market share among specialties. Possible antitrust risk if above 30% share.
- Solutions: Limit the practitioners included in joint contractual offerings in the danger areas or merge into an integrated, risk-sharing entity.

Group Boycott

If the group does include a provision to exclude other practitioners in joint contract offerings, then group boycott may be an issue. This issue is typically raised by payers that fear there has been collaboration on the part of many practices to force them not to sign a standard contract. If provider groups are working together in some form of joint venture relationship, care must be take to ensure that each group is free to sign and negotiate contracts with payers.

Tying

Payers and competitors that accuse providers of "tying" services cite providers' use of market power in one area to affect customers to purchase services in another area. In the mental health arena, tying might occur if a group represents a significant market share in a certain specialty and is contracting with a provider hospital. If consumers of mental health services cannot obtain the services of one entity without the other, allegations of tying may exist. Unlike the other antitrust issues, developing a fully integrated model will not solve this problem because single corporations can engage in this illegal activity. To eliminate this risk, hire an outside consultant to determine each entity's market power according to the following rules:

- Determine market share for practitioners (as a whole and by specialty). Market power usually exists at 30-35% market share.
- Likewise, review the hospital's market share to determine if market power exists.

If market power exists in any of the areas, break the provider–hospital ties in that area and offer payers the option to chose either the hospital's services, the provider's, or both. The offer of separate or combined services is enough to prevent antitrust tying problems.

Antitrust concerns are of little concern in fully integrated systems of care where a single parent organization assumes financial risk for provision of services. Group practices seem to be most at-risk in relationships where no financial risk is at stake. Providers are encouraged, where there is doubt, to seek appropriate counsel from a qualified attorney, the Federal Trade Commission, or the Department of Justice.

SUMMARY

This chapter presents a summary of business entities and their various tax and legal advantages and disadvantages. The difficulty in selecting an entity comes in balancing the needs it must serve: income tax benefits, business law planning, limitation of personal and group liability, and organizational structure that allows for effective management and government. This chapter has intentionally been presented last to force practitioners to work through developing group practice goals and business objectives. Once those are firmly established, an attorney qualified in this area can guide you to the best organization that meets the group's needs.

8

Group Formation Checklist

THIS LIST IS INTENDED *to focus on critical issues in group practice formation. It may not be comprehensive and the reader is cautioned not to consider items in isolation—the questions are interrelated. Patient management decisions, for example, may drive financial management as well as operational issues.*

GROUP FORMATION ISSUES

1. Do the merging groups share a similar treatment philosophy?
2. What are each groups goals for a successful merger?
3. Can the individual psychologists practice together?
4. Can the groups reach compromises on financial and practice development decisions?
5. Do practitioners respect each other's patient management style?
6. Would a practitioner consider referring a patient to another in the group?
7. Are there any integrity issues either group should consider?
8. How will the merging groups integrate new associates or partners?
9. Will seniority influence member compensation?
10. Will specialty experience influence member compensation?
11. Have policies been established concerning professional courtesy, employee health, and members' income from sources other that the group?
12. Have member benefits been determined?

This list is an adaptation of the American Group Practice Association's 1978 publication *Group Practice: Guidelines to Forming or Joining a Medical Group.*

13. Are group norms incompatible with each other? Is this an issue that cannot be resolved?
14. How is the leadership chosen in each organization?
15. Is each group's cohesiveness such that a merger would be considered a threat?

ORGANIZATIONAL ISSUES

16. Why are we building this practice?
17. What are the group's financial goals? Professional goals?
18. Is the group risk-averse?
19. How does the group see itself in a managed care environment?
20. What market changes in the future should affect decisions now?
21. Are goals among practitioners mutually exclusive or somewhat compatible?
22. Is there a market for this group practice that is capable of supporting our individual and group goals?
23. What value should be placed on each group's assets and liabilities?
24. Have the patient and payer demands, group resources, and resultant cash flows been projected to predict group success?
25. Has the patient's/payer's method of payment (fee for service, prepayment) been agreed upon?
26. Has the basis for establishing the fee schedule (third party schedules, cost of services, relative value studies, etc.) been agreed upon?
27. Has a long range plan been established for the clinic facility and site?
28. Will the clinic facility be newly constructed, leased, or will an existing structure be renovated for clinic use?
29. Will a facility feasibility study be performed?
30. Has an organizational structure for the building program been agreed upon? Who will preside over this organizational structure?
31. Has a specific site been selected? Will the land be purchased or leased? Have facility and land cost estimates been acquired and capital needs determined?
32. Has interim and long-term facility financing been acquired and under what terms and conditions?
33. Is the site location convenient to the medical staff and patients? Has consideration been given to site access, landscaping, parking, utilities, and zoning?

34. Which planning and construction approach (traditional design, build, or turnkey) has been chosen by the group?
35. Have the merging parties developed a comprehensive business plan? Have all members approved its contents?
36. Have the goals and objectives been established and documented by group members?
37. Do these goals and/or their objectives consider personal convenience, practice economics, professional development, and/or behavioral health services?
38. Have the strategies been established to accomplish the defined group objectives?
39. Have the goals, objectives, and strategies been tested for internal consistency?

OPERATIONS ISSUES

40. Have group strategies been translated into operating professional, administrative, and patient care policies?
41. Has an organizational structure or chart been determined as a result of the policy development process?
42. Has a communications system/plan been established?
43. What type of telephone system has been agreed upon?
44. Will the dictating system be centralized, decentralized, or a combination of these?
45. Will the dictating system interface with the telephone system?
46. Have decisions been made concerning copying, facsimile, mail handling, paging, and intercom systems?
47. Will a patient/payer information booklet or brochure be published?
48. Have policies been formulated to guide and integrate the various communications subsystems?
49. Have decisions been made on the amount of information and the method of its collection at patient registration?
50. Is patient preregistration planned?
51. Will a health history questionnaire be initiated at patient registration? Has it been prepared?
52. How will the office deal with filing claims on behalf of numerous carriers?
53. Will patient identification cards be used? Will they be embossed?

54. Will the registration process be centralized, decentralized, or a combination of these?
55. Will the medical record be initiated during patient registration?
56. Are there any plans to invest in a paperless medical records system?
57. Has a services time interval been agreed upon for appointments? Will each staff member's interval be unique to his practice?
58. Are the appointment and reception activities to be performed by the same clinic personnel?
59. Have policies been established for intraclinic referrals, referrals to and from external sources, hospital referrals, and referral reports and consultations?
60. Have agreements been made concerning the patient information to be housed in the medical record? The order of the record itself and the progress notes? The procedural and diagnostic codes to be used? The hospital information to be contained in the record? Ancillary reports and their sequencing?
61. Has a medical records jacket been agreed upon?
62. Will the medical record files be centralized, decentralized, or a combination of these?
63. Which type of filing system (alphabetical, straight numerical, terminal digit, etc.) will be used?
64. Will the records be color coded?
65. Has the method of record storage (file cabinets, open shelves, combination of these, etc.) been determined?
66. Has a chart requisition and transportation system been established?
67. Will record cross-indexes be needed?
68. Will records be pulled in order of requisition receipt or time of appointment?
69. Have policies been established concerning record maintenance and release? Record retention? Records purging?
70. Will the method of recording charges be centralized, decentralized, or a combination of these?
71. Has policy been established to guide the insurance processing activities of the group?
72. Have policies been established for purchasing, supply, inventory, and maintenance?
73. Has policy been established to integrate the purchasing, receiving, inventory, and accounts payable activities?
74. Has policy been agreed upon to control maintenance, grounds keep-

ing, housekeeping, security, and vehicle maintenance and use activities?
75. Will an orientation be established for all new employees?
76. Will job descriptions be prepared for all positions in the clinic?
77. Has policy been established regarding wage and salary administration?
78. Will a personnel policies handbook/manual be prepared?
79. What are the MIS requirements of the group?
80. Has consensus been reached about the level of MIS sophistication?
81. Have policies been established on the MIS requirements and evaluation?
82. Have the specific statistics required for internal management been agreed upon?
83. Have policies been established to ensure the collection and reporting of information necessary to measure and evaluate the quality of care?
84. Has the patient space been satisfactorily designed?
85. Have the clinical and administrative control areas been designed?
86. Have staff areas been satisfactorily designed?
87. Will there be an immediate care or walk-in area?
88. Is the design of the administration and office space satisfactory?

FINANCING CONSIDERATIONS AND FINANCIAL MANAGEMENT ISSUES

89. Has a financial plan been established? What business year is to be used?
90. If prospective group members were already practicing in the community, has a method been determined to merge individual assets pertaining to their practice into the organization?
91. Have cash management and control policies been established?
92. Has an accounting method been chosen and a chart of accounts established?
93. Have the balance sheet and incomes statement items and their format been agreed upon?
94. Have the books of account (journals and ledgers) been established?
95. Have accounts receivable, credit, and collections policies and procedures been established?
96. Has a budget been established?

97. Have audit policies and procedures been agreed upon?
98. Have salary ranges and levels been established for non-practitioner employees?
99. Is the salary structure competitive in the local market?
100. Have employee benefits been agreed upon?
101. Has an income distribution arrangement for practitioner compensation been agreed upon?
102. Will practitioner salaries be adjusted according to uncollectibles or plan membership variances?
103. Have credit and collections policies been established?
104. Has a billing schedule been agreed upon?
105. Will the group own or lease the facility?

GOVERNANCE

106. Have articles of incorporation/agreement been drawn and has proper distribution been made?
107. Have the bylaws been drawn and has proper distribution been made?
108. Have the decisions been made concerning the governance of the group?
109. Have officers and key staff to be employed by the organization been selected?
110. Will advisory committees be necessary? If so, in which area?
111. How will the board of directors be structured? The executive committee? What will their duties encompass?

LEGAL AND STRUCTURAL CONSIDERATIONS

112. Has an organizational form been chosen for the medical practice (sole proprietorship, partnership, limited liability company, regular or S corporation)?
113. Have potential antitrust implications been addressed?
114. Has a budget been established for any necessary outside counsel—tax, legal, consulting?
115. How will consultants be used in the group development process, if at all?
116. If the facility is to be owned by the group, has the organizational form for ownership been determined (sole proprietorship, partnership, limited liability company, regular or S corporation)?

Glossary

For your convenience, the following is a list of key terms. Other terms are defined in the text where appropriate.

ACCESS   Patients' ability to obtain needed health services. Measures of access include the location of health facilities and their hours of operation, patient travel time and distance to health facilities, the availability of medical services, and the cost of care.

ACUTE CARE   Health care provided to treat conditions that are short term or episodic in nature.

ANCILLARY SERVICES   Inpatient hospital services other than bed, board, and nursing care; for example, drugs, dressings, operating room services, special diets, X-rays, laboratory examination, anesthesia, medications, etc.

AVERAGE LENGTH OF STAY (ALOS)   Number of days a patient customarily remains an inpatient for a specified diagnosis or procedure; used in precertification and recertification procedures.

CAPITATION   A method of payment for health care services in which the provider accepts a fixed amount of payment per subscriber, per period of time, in return for providing specified services over a specified period of time.

CARRIER   any commercial insurance company.

CARVE OUT   An arrangement in which coverage for a specific category of services (e.g., mental health/substance abuse, vision care, prescription drugs) is provided through a contract with a separate set of providers. The contract with these providers may specify certain payment and utilization management arrangements.

CASE MANAGEMENT   The monitoring, planning, and coordination of treatment rendered to patients with conditions expected to require high cost or extensive services. Case management is focused and longitudinal, usually following the member for 3-6 months minimum to avoid readmission.

CASE MANAGER   A generic term for various professionals who perform different case management functions, usually working with clients, families, providers, and insurers to coordinate all services deemed necessary to provide the client with a plan of medically necessary and appropriate health care.

CHAMPUS   Civilian Health and Medical Program of the Uniformed Services. A health plan of vast size with beneficiaries in all states, and a natural field experiment in the use of mental health fee for services practices. The patterns of use have major public policy implications for consumers' access, providers' availability, the cost of alternatives to hospitalization, extent of use, and quality of care.

CLAIMS REVIEW   A review of claims by government, medical foundations, Professional Review Organizations, insurers, or others responsible for payment to determine liability and amount of payment.

COINSURANCE   The cost-sharing ratio between a health plan participant and the insurer or employer, Frequently, the participant is responsible for 20% of covered charges and the insurer or employer will pay 80% copayment.

CONCURRENT   REVIEW A third party review of the medical necessity, level of care, length of stay, appropriateness of services, and discharge planning for patients in health care facilities. Occurs at the time the patient is being treated.

CONTINUUM OF CARE   In behavioral health, generally defined as the spectrum of care delivered in residential treatment, inpatient, partial hospitalization, home health, and outpatient settings.

COPAYMENT   A type of cost sharing whereby insured or covered persons pay a specified flat amount per unit of service or unit of time (e.g., $10 per visit, $25 per inpatient hospital day); insurance covers the remainder of the cost.

COST CONTAINMENT   Actions taken by employers and insurers to curtail health care costs, e.g., increasing employee cost sharing, requiring second opinions, or preadmission screening.

COST SHARING   Requirement that health care consumers contribute to their own medical care costs through deductibles and coinsurance or copayments.

COVERED EXPENSE (OR COVERED BENEFIT)   Health care costs that are specifically cited as reimbursable by the health plan.

CREDENTIALING   The process of reviewing a practitioner's credentials—i.e., training, experience, or demonstrated ability—for the purpose of determining if criteria for clinical privileging are met.

DAYS/1,000/YEAR   This is a common utilization measurement used in the health care industry that refers to a ratio of the number of days a patient population has for a particular service, per 1,000 members enrolled for a given year. For example, if an HMO with 10,000 members experiences 3,800 total hospital days, the relevant ratio is 380 hospital days per 1,000 members per year.

DAY TREATMENT   Intensive care provided on a partial-day basis.

DEDUCTIBLE   Flat sum that must be paid by the patient/employee before an insurer assumes liability for all or part of the remaining cost of covered services. A deductible is most commonly used in major medical policies.

DIAGNOSTIC RELATED GROUPS (DRGS)   A reimbursement methodology whereby hospitals receive a fixed fee per patient based on the admitting diagnosis regardless of length of stay or amount of service received.

DISCHARGE PLANNING   Process of identifying, monitoring, counseling, and arranging follow-up care of hospitalized patients. Usually performed by social workers or nurses, the process ensures patients receive appropriate counseling and follow-up care to assist their convalescence and keep hospital stays at a minimum.

EMPLOYEE ASSISTANCE PROGRAM (EAP)   An employer's program of counseling and other forms of assistance to employees experiencing alcoholism or other substance abuse, or emotional and family problems.

ENROLLMENT   The means by which a person or persons establish membership in a group insurance plan.

ERISA   The Employee Retirement Income Security Act of 1974, P.L. 93-406, was enacted to protect employee pension funds and to encourage the development of other employee benefit plans, including health benefit plans. ERISA has a profound effect on the ability of states to regulate health insurance, employee benefit plans, and other related matters.

EXCESS CHARGES   The portion of any charge greater than the usual and prevailing charge for a service. A charge is "usual and prevailing" when it does not exceed the typical charge of the provider in the absence of insurance and is no greater than the general level of charges for comparable services and supplies made by other providers in the same area.

EXCLUSIVE PROVIDER ORGANIZATION (EPO)   EPOs are similar to PPOs in their organization and purpose. However, beneficiaries covered by an EPO are required to receive all of their covered services from providers that participate in the EPO. The EPO does not cover services received from other providers. Some EPOs parallel HMOs in that they not only require exclusive use of the EPO provider network, but also use a "gatekeeper" approach to authorize nonprimary care services.

EXPLANATION OF BENEFITS (EOB)   A form provided to patients (and providers) after a claim has been paid; useful in enabling the patient to check not only benefits received but also the services for which the provider has requested compensation. In Medicare, called Explanation of Medical benefits (EOMB).

FEE FOR SERVICE   In the traditional fee for service model, the provider bills the consumer or payer for a specified amount, typically on the basis of the amount of time spent delivering the service. Until recently, the provider determined the fee charged for the service and customary fees were generally accepted. Now, the provider may be required to accept a payer's fee schedule, which demands a certain fee be accepted as payment in full. PPOs represent an attempt to save the fee for service method of payment by regulating the cost of treatment in the context of a traditional reimbursement plan.

FEE SCHEDULE   A listing of accepted fees or predetermined monetary allowances for specified services and procedures.

FREE-STANDING FACILITY   A health care center that is physically separated from a hospital or other institution of which it is a legal part or with which it is affiliated, or an independently operated or owned private or public business or enterprise providing a limited health care service or range such as ambulatory surgery, hemodialysis treatment, diagnostic tests or examinations, etc.

GATEKEEPING   The process by which a primary care provider directly provides the primary patient care and coordinates all diagnostic testing and specialty referrals required for a patient's medical care. Referrals must be prior-authorized by the "gatekeeper" unless there is an emergency. Gatekeeping is a subset of the functions of the primary provider case manger.

GROUP CONTRACT   An arrangement between the managed care company and the subscribing group containing rates, performance covenants, relationships among parties, schedule of benefits, and other conditions. The term is generally limited to a 12 month period but may be renewed.

GROUP HEALTH INSURANCE   A single program insuring a group of associated individuals against financial loss resulting from illness or injury.

GROUP MODEL HMO   An HMO that contracts with a primary care or multispecialty group practice for the delivery of health services.

GROUP PRACTICE   The organization of a group of practitioners as a private partnership, limited liability company, or corporation; participating practitioners share facilities and personnel as well as earnings from their practice. The providers comprising the practice may represent either a single specialty or a range of behavioral health specialties.

HEALTH CARE FINANCING ADMINISTRATION (HCFA)   The federal agency within the U.S. Department of Health and Human Services responsible for administering the Medicare program.

HEALTH MAINTENANCE ORGANIZATION (HMO)   A health care delivery system that provides comprehensive health services to an enrolled population frequently for a prepaid, fixed (capitated) payment although other payment arrangements can be made. The organization consists of a network of health care providers rendering a wide range of health services and assumes the financial risk of providing these services. Enrollees generally will not be reimbursed for care provided outside the HMO network.

HOLD HARMLESS CLAUSE   A clause frequently found in managed care contracts whereby the HMO and the provider hold each other not liable for malpractice or corporate malfeasance if either of the parties is found to be liable. Many insurance carriers exclude this type of liability from coverage. It may also refer to language that prohibits the provider from billing patients if their managed care company becomes insolvent. State and federal regulations may require this language.

INDEMNITY INSURANCE PLAN   An insurance plan that pays specific dollar amounts to the insured individual for specific services and procedures without guaranteeing complete coverage for the full cost of health care services.

INDIVIDUAL PRACTICE ASSOCIATION (IPA) MODEL HMO   An organization that contracts with individual health care professionals to provide services in their own offices for enrollees of a health plan. The specialists are generally paid on a fee for service basis but primary care providers may receive capitated payments.

INTEGRATED CARE   An alternative delivery system developed by the American Psychological Association as a response to the rising costs of providing health care services. Based on six concepts: Benefit Design, Case Management and Utilization Review, Communications, Direct Contracting, Network Development, and Outcomes.

MANAGED CARE   A means of providing health care services within a defined network of health care providers who are given the responsibility to manage and provide quality, cost-effective care. Increasingly, the term is being used by many analysts to include (in addition to HMOs) PPOs and even forms of indemnity insurance coverage that incorporate preadmission certifications and other utilization controls.

MANDATED BENEFITS   Specific treatments, providers, or individuals required by law to be included in commercial health plans.

MARKET SHARE   That part of the market potential that a managed care company has captured, usually market share is expressed as a percentage of the market potential.

MEDICAID   The federally financed, state-run health care program for the poor.

MEDICARE   Title XVIII of the Social Security Act that provides benefits to citizens aged 65 and older and to the disabled; Part A covers hospitalization, extended care, and nursing home care; Part B provides medical-surgical benefits.

MENTAL HEALTH AND DRUG ABUSE SERVICES   There are three basic types of mental health services: inpatient care provided in short term psychiatric beds in a general hospital or in specialized psychiatric facilities; outpatient care for individual or group counseling; partial hospitalization, a combination of both of the above. Also see Employee Assistance Program.

MSO   An entity that usually contracts with practitioner groups, Independent Practice Associations, and medical foundations to provide a range of services required in medical practices, such as accounting, utilization review, and staffing.

MULTISPECIALTY GROUP   A group of doctors who represent various specialties and who work together in a group practice.

NETWORK   A group of providers that mutually contract with carriers or employers to provide health care services to participants in a specified managed care plan. The contract determines the payment method and rates, utilization controls, and target utilization rates by plan participants.

NETWORK MODEL   An organizational form in which the HMO contracts for medical services within a "network" of medical groups. HealthNet, a Blue Cross sponsored HMO serving southern California, is an example of a network model. For federal qualification purposes, such models are designated as IPAs.

OUT OF AREA BENEFITS   The coverage allowed to HMO members for emergency situations outside of the prescribed geographic area of the HMO.

OUT OF AREA CARE   Care received by an HMO's enrollees when they are outside the HMO's geographic territory. Services received are usually not prearranged by the HMO.

PEER REVIEW   Evaluation by practicing providers (or other qualified professionals) of the quality and efficiency of services ordered or performed by other practicing providers. Peer review is the all-inclusive term for medical review efforts. Medical practice, inpatient hospital and extended care facility analyses, utilization review, medical audit, ambulatory care, and claims review are all aspects of peer review.

PER DIEM   The negotiated daily rate for delivery of all inpatient hospital services provided in one day regardless of the actual services provided. Per diems can also be developed by the type of care provided, e.g., one per diem rate for adult mental health, a different rate for adolescent substance abuse treatment, etc.

PERFORMANCE STANDARDS   Standards an individual provider is expected to meet, especially with respect to quality of care. The standards may define volume of care delivered per time period.

POOL   A large number of small groups or individuals that are analyzed and rated as a single large group for insurance purposes. A risk pool may be any account that attempts to find the claims liability for a group with a common denominator.

PREADMISSION REVIEW   When a provider requests that a patient be hospitalized, another opinion may be sought. The second provider reviews the treatment plan, evaluates the patient's condition, and confirms the request for admission or recommends another course of action. Similar to second opinions on surgery.

PREAUTHORIZATION   Review and approval of covered benefits, based on a provider's treatment plan. Some insurers require preauthorization for certain high cost procedures. Other insurers apply the preauthorization requirement when charges are in excess of a specified dollar amount.

PRECERTIFICATION   A review of the necessity and length of a recommended hospital stay. Certification prior to admission is often required for all non-emergencies and certification within 48 hours following admission for emergency treatment.

PREEXISTING CONDITION   Any condition for which charges have been incurred during a specified period of time just prior to the effective date of an insurance policy. Frequently, a contract with a different insurer will not cover the preexisting conditions of employees or their dependents.

PREFERRED PROVIDER ORGANIZATION   Selective contracting agreement with a specified network of health care providers at reduced or negotiated payment rates. In exchange for reduced rates, providers frequently receive expedited claims payment and/or a reasonably predictable market share. Employees have financial incentives to utilize PPO providers.

PROVIDER   Any health care professional (or facility) licensed to provide one or more health care services to patients.

QUALITY ASSURANCE   Activities and programs intended to ensure the quality of care in a defined medical setting or program. Such programs include methods for documenting clinical practice, educational components intended to remedy identified deficiencies in quality, the components necessary to identify and correct such deficiencies (such as peer or utilization review), and a formal process to assess the program's own effectiveness.

QUALITY MANAGEMENT   A participative intervention in which all employees and managers continuously review the quality of the service they provide. The process used identifies problems, tests solutions to those problems, and constantly monitors the solutions for improvement.

RATING   The process of determining rates or the cost of insurance for individuals, groups, or classes of risks.

RESIDENTIAL CARE   Care provided in a residential treatment center or group home on a 24-hour-a-day basis.

RISK   The chance or possibility of loss. The sharing of risk is often employed as a utilization control mechanism within the HMO setting. Risk is often defined in insurance terms as the possibility of loss associated with a given population.

RISK POOL   A poll of money that is to be used for defined expenses. Commonly, if the money that is put at risk is not expended by the end of the year, some or all of it is returned to those managing the risk.

SELECTIVE CONTRACTING   Negotiation by third party payers of a limited number of contracts with health care professionals and facilities in a given service area. Preferential reimbursement practices and/or benefits are then offered to patients seeking care from these providers.

SELF-FUNDING   A procedure whereby a firm uses its own funds to pay claims, rather than transferring the financial risks of paying claims to an outside insurer in exchange for premium payment. Also referred to as self-insurance. Insurance companies and other third party administrator organizations may be engaged to process claims or the self-insured company may choose to handle its own. Four forms of claims administration are common:

COST PLUS   Third party pays claims and bills the employer for the actual amount of claims in a month (cost) plus an administrative fee to a carrier (plus).

ADMINISTRATIVE SERVICES ONLY (ASO)   Employer contracts with a firm to handle claims and make payments for billed services.

SELF-ADMINISTRATION   Employer takes on the risk for claims and does the administrative work involved in paying claims.

MINIMUM PREMIUM PLAN   Insurance company provides aggregate stop-loss protection plus claims adminstration services.

STAFF MODEL HMO   An HMO in which professional providers within a multispecialty group are salaried employees of the HMO.

STOP-LOSS COVERAGE   Insurance for a self-insured plan that reimburses the company for any losses it might incur in its health claims beyond a specified amount.

THIRD PARTY ADMINISTRATOR (TPA)   Outside company responsible for handling claims and performing administrative tasks associated with health insurance plan maintenance.

THIRD PARTY PAYER   Any organization that pays or insures health care expenses on behalf of beneficiaries or recipients who pay premiums for such coverage.

USUAL, CUSTOMARY, AND REASONABLE (UCR)   Health insurance plans that pay a provider's full charge if it is reasonable and does not exceed his or her usual charges and the amount customarily charged for service by other providers in the area.

UTILIZATION REVIEW   An independent determination of whether health care services are appropriate and medically necessary on a prospective, concurrent, and/or retrospective basis to ensure that appropriate and necessary health care services are provided. UR is frequently used to curtail the provision of inappropriate services and/or to ensure that services are provided in the most cost-effective manner.

Bibliography

Ackerman, K. (1993). The role of the physician in executive management. *Medical Group Management Journal, 40*(5), 67–76.

Addleman, R. (1994). Governing board, know thyself: A technique for self-assessment. *Trustee, 47,* 24–25.

Aeschleman, M., & Koch, A. (1993). Independent practice associations: Risk contracting, financial controls and processes. *Medical Group Management Journal, 40*(4), 70–84.

Bader, B. S. (1994). Physician involvement in the governance of integrated systems. *Health System Leader, 1*(3), 4–14.

Bader, B. S., & Matheny, M. (1994). Understanding capitation and at-risk contracting. *Health System Leader, 1*(1), 4–16.

Balsamo, R. R., & Pine, M. (1994). Twelve questions to ask about your outcomes monitoring system: Part I. *Physician Executive, 20*(4), 13–17.

Balsamo, R. R., & Pine, M. (1994). Twelve questions to ask about your outcomes monitoring system: Part II. *Physician Executive, 20*(5), 22–25.

Barlow, J. (1994). Practice parameters and outcomes measurement: Managing for quality. *Medical Group Management Journal, 41*(1), 12–17.

Barnett, A. E., & Mayer, T. (1993). HMO performance assessment: Group practice strategies and considerations. *Managed Care Quarterly, 1*(1), 1–18.

Batalden, P. B., et al. (1994). Linking outcomes measurement to continual inprovement: The serial "V" way of thinking about improving clinical care. *The Joint Commission Journal on Quality Improvement, 20*(4), 167–180.

Beck, L. C. (1992). The key to successful group practice. *The Physician's Advisory, 92*(6), 8.

Bell, C., & Zelly, M. (1993). Successful implementation of Medicare risk contracting. *Medical Group Management Journal, 40*(4), 86–94.

Bender, A. D., & Dawes, E. (1994). Understanding practice costs: A critical step to negotiating capitation. *The Journal of Medical Practice Management, 10*(2), 4–16.

Benvenuto, J. A., et al. (1991). From 12 solo practices to a hospital-based LMSG in 100 easy steps. *Medical Group Management Journal, 38*(4), 84–92.

Bergman, R. (1994). Getting the goods on guidelines. *Hospitals and Health Networks, 6*(20), 70–74.

Brayer, K. A., & Scroggins, E. S. (1993). How to approach managed care contracting in the 1990s. *Medical Group Management Journal, 40*(2), 70–74.

Caesar, N. B. (1994). How to gain leverage with a health plan. *Medical Economics, 71*(3), 32–47.

Caesar, N. B., & Grab, E. L. (1993). Negotiating profitable managed care contracts for your group. *Group Practice Journal, 42*(5), 31–32.

Chodroff, C., & Krivenko, C. A. (1994). The analysis of clinical outcomes: Getting started in benchmarking. *The Joint Commission Journal on Quality Improvement, 20*(5), 260–266.

Choosing and contracting with managed care organizations (1993). *The Physician's Advisory, Special Supplement,* 4-6.

Coit, R. B. (1994). A simplified approach to clinical practice guidelines. *Group Practice Journal, 43*(4), 45–48.

Coopers & Lybrand, L.L.P. (1994). *Choosing a business entity in the 1990's.* Washington, DC: Author.

Coyne, J. S., & Simon, S. D. (1994). Is your organization ready to share financial risk with HMOs? *Healthcare Financial News, 48*(8), 30–34.

Damsey, J. L., & Owen, A. Practice X reads between the lines. *Family Practice Management, 1*(4), 41–48.

D'Antuono, R. (1994). Transition to capitation: Assessing your organizational readiness. *GFP Notes, 7*(2), 8–12.

Davies, A. R., et al. Outcomes assessment in clinical settings: A consensus statement on principles and best practices in project management. *The Joint Commission Journal on Quality Improvement, 20*(1), 6–16.

DeMuth, D. L. (1992). Pros and cons of incorporating your practice. *Physician's Management, 32*(6), 197–210.

Donabedian, A. (1992). The role of outcomes in quality assessment and assurance. *Quality Review Bulletin, 18*(11), 356–360.

Driscoll, T. L., & Schieble, M. T. (1993). Tax exemptions criteria for integrated delivery systems. *Health Care Law Newsletter, 8*(10), 14–19.

Edelman, N. (1994). Creating an integrated group practice. *GFP Notes, 7*(2), 1–7.

Enders, R. J. (1993). Antitrust laws: Considerations but not barriers to integration. *Health Care Law Newsletter, 8*(10), 20–27.

Erdlen, F. R. (1992). How to analyze outcomes measurements. *Personnel Journal, 71*(10), 107–111.

Fahey, P. S. (1994). Outcomes research: It's not just for academia. *Medical Group Management Journal, 41*(3), 16–72.

Farmer, A., & Tosa, M. E. Using cost accounting data to develop capitation rates. *Topics in Health Care Financing, 21*(1), 1–12.

Fehey, D. F. (1994). Professional oligarchy in medical group practice: Toward the development of a middle-range theory. *The Journal of Ambulatory Care Management, 17*(1), 77–90.

Feltham, J. (1993). AGPA builds national database on patient outcomes. *Group Practice Journal, 42*(4), 22–35.

Gaus, C. R. (1994). Clinical practice guidelines: Paths to quality care. *Group Practice Journal, 43*(5), 60–65.

Golembesky, H. (1992). A future model for integrated health care. *Medical Group Management Journal, 39*(4), 96–104.

Grayson, J. C. (1993). Outcomes, benchmarking and TQM. *Health Systems Review, 26*(6), 6–16.

Guadagnoli, E., & McNeil, B. J. (1994). Outcomes research: Hope for the future or the latest rage? *Inquiry, 31*(1), 14–24.

Hadorn, D., et al. (1994). Making judgments about treatment effectiveness based on health outcomes: Theoretical and practice issues. *The Joint Commission Journal on Quality Improvement, 20*(10), 547-554.

Handley, M. R., et al. (1994). An evidence-based approach to evaluating and improving clinical practice: Implementing practice guidelines. *HMO Practice, 8*(2), 75–83.

Handley, M. R., & Stuart, M. E. (1994). An evidence-based approach to evaluating and improving clinical practice: Guideline development. *HMO Practice, 8*(1), 10–19.

Harlan, D. (1995). The implications of practice guidelines for physician medical malpractice liability. *Physician Executive, 20*(5), 20–21.

Harris, D. G., et al. The transformation and progression of physician organizations. *Medical Group Management Update, 33*(2), 10–12.

Hastings, D. A., & Temchine, D. D. E. (1993). Current legal considerations in the formation of group practice. *Group Practice Journal, 42*(1), 81–85.

Henderson-Damon, C., & Owen, A. (1994). Practice X looks at managed care. *Family Practice Management, 1*(3), 53–61.

Hope for the future, tools for success (1994). *Medical Group Management Journal, 41*(1), 18–23.

Is there an "LSO" in your future? Here's what it is, how to set it up (1993). *The Physician's Advisory, 93*(6), 1–2.

Jahnke, M. D., & Sullivan, T. L. (1993). Medical practice management trends: Evaluating managed care arrangements. *Journal of Medical Practice Management, 7*(2), 90–93.

Johnson, B. A., & Niederman, G. A. (1994). Integrated provider networks, a primer. *Medical Group Management Journal, 41*(6), 62–68.

Johnson, R. E. (1993). Practice guidelines: Efficacy and implementation in HMOs. *HMO Practice, 7*(3), 119–121.

Jones, K. (1992). Specialty groups "doing battle" to survive. *Medical Group Management Journal, 39*(4), 90–94.

Jones, T. C. (1994). *Planning for the future: Moving to the multispecialty group organizational structure.* Englewood, CO: Fellow American College of Medical Professional Executives (FACMPE).

Karp, D. (1994). Avoiding managed care's liability risks. *Medical Economics, 71*(8), 68–72.

Kibbe, D. C. (1994). Integrating guidelines with continuous quality improvement: Doing the right thing the right way to achieve the right goals. *The Joint Commission Journal on Quality Improvement, 20*(4), 181–190.

Knuth, K. L. (1994). Reorganizing of a medical professional corporation and a building corporation. *College Review, 11*(1), 25–30.

Koemptgen, J. M. (1991). Organizational conflict: Strong department heads versus central administration. *The College Review, 8*(1), 56–61.

Kongsvedt, P. R. (1993). *The managed care handbook* (2nd ed.). Gaithersburg, Maryland: Aspen.

Kurtz, M. E. (1992). A discussion of group practice governance issues. *Medical Group Management Journal, 39*(5), 46-52.

Lake, D. B. (1993). Point-of-service plans—The risks and rewards. *Medical Group Management Journal, 40*(4), 36–37.

Larkin, H. (1994). Limit your downside. *American Medical News, 40*(37), 29–31.

Lindeke, J. M. (1992). The "Foundation Model" as a hospital-physician organizational structure: Panacea, fad, or ...? *Health Care Law Newsletter, 7*(2), 9–12.

Lindeke, J. M. (1993). Structural and legal issues in the formation of integrated delivery systems. *Health Care Law Newsletter, 8*(10), 5–14.

Longo, D. R. (1994). The impact of outcomes management on the hospital-physician relationship. *Topics in Health Care Financing, 20*(4), 36–74.

MacDonald, A. S. (1991). Clinical practice governance. *GFP Notes, 4*(4), i–iv.

MacDonald, A. S. (1994). Integrating management of physician groups and hospitals. *Topics in Health Care Financing, 20*(4), 48–54.

Mack, J. M. (1992). Are open-ended or point of service plans right for you? *Medical Group Management Journal, 39*(1), 32-38.

Maddon, D. (1994). Getting paid what you're worth. *The Internist, 35*(7), 6–9.

McGee-Cory, J. A. (1992). Criteria for determining medical practice management skills requirements: A case study. *The College Review, 9*(1), 5–19.

Miller, J. L. (1993). The changing role of the group medical director. *Integrated Healthcare Reports, 1*(7), 10–12.

Miller, J. N. (1993, February). Forming a medical group: What you need to know to get started. *California Physician*, 50–56.

Miller, W. (1993). Legal considerations in managed care contracting. *Topics in Health Care Financing, 20*(2), 17–25.

Mitchell, P. H. (1993). Perspectives in outcome-oriented care systems. *Nursing Administration Quarterly, 17*(3), 1–7.

Montague, J. (1994). Do-it-yourself outcomes. *Hospitals and Health Networks, 68*(13), 42–44.

Moody, S. R. (1994). The changing environment for academic practice. *GFP Notes, 7*(3), 10–13.

Moran, G. F. (1993). Rate structuring in managed care contracts demands detailed information. *Medical Group Management Journal, 40*(4), 9–10.

Oberman, L. (1993). How to get doctors in line with clinical guidelines. *American Medical News, 36*(29), 10–11.

Organizational readiness for capitation: A self assessment. (1994). *GFP Notes, 7*(2), 16–17.

Ottensmeyer, D. J. Governance of the integrated health care system: A new governance issue for group practice. *Group Practice Journal, 42*(1), 12–16.

Owen, A. (1993). Managed care plans: How many can your practice handle? *Family Practice Management, 1*(1), 95–103.

Pavlock, E. J. (1994). *Financial management for medical groups: A primer for new managers and a refresher for the experienced.* Reston, VA: Center for Research in Ambulatory Health Care Administration.

Peter, C. L. (1994). *Evolution of leadership.* Englewood, CO: FACMPE.

Peter, C. L. (1994). *Planning for future directions.* Englewood, CO: FACMPE.

Pollard, J. W. (1994). *The Physician Manager in Group Practice.* Englewood, CO: Center for Research in Ambulatory Health Care Financing.

Pope, C. (1994). Time to start studying: Report cards are coming. *Medical Group Management Update, 32*(2), 10–12.

Rea, D. K. (1990). The advanced group practice model. *The College Review, 7*(1), 25–37.

Rosenfield, R. H. (1994). Replacing the workshop model. *Topics in Health Care Financing, 20*(4), 1–15.

Sanderson-Austin, J. (1994). An outcomes measurement study primer. *Group Practice Journal, 43*(4), 14–20.

Schlichting, E. S. (1993). *Good board members are made not born.* Englewood, CO: FACMPE.

Shiffman, R. N. (1993). Clinical guidelines in medical practice. *Journal of Medical Practice Management, 9*(2), 70–74.

Signorelli, T. F. (1994). Implementing and managing organizational change in medical groups. *College Review, 11*(1), 5–24.

Steinwachs, D. M. (1994). How will outcomes measurement work? *Health Affairs, 13*(4), 153–162.

Stevens, S. Research a health plan's fiscal fitness before signing contract, experts warn. *Physicians Financial News, 10*(4), 10.

Tavantis, T. N., et al. (1994). Introducing teamwork in physician groups: A case study. *Medical Group Management Journal, 41*(2), 62–80.

Thomasson, G. O. (1994). Participatory risk management: Promoting physician compliance with practice guidelines. *The Joint Commission Journal on Quality Improvement, 20*(6), 317–329.

Travis, R. D. (1991). Effective committees: A contradiction in terms? *Medical Group Management Journal, 38*(2), 24–29.

Two checklists can give offices the upper hand in managed care contracts (1994). *Medical Office Manager, 8*(1), 11–12.

Tulli, C. G. (1992). *The age of the medical group practice bureaucracy.* Englewood, CO: FACMPE.

Unland, J. J. (1993). *Group practice options: From medical corporations to clinics without walls.* Chicago: American Medical Association.

Venable, S. R. (1994). Quality and outcomes measurement: Facilitating optimal results with caring and technology. *Managed Care Medicine, 1*(4), 12–16.

Vogel, D. E. (1993). *The physician and managed care.* Chicago: American Medical Association.

Votek, A. (1994). How to evaluate a capitated offer. *OBG Management, 6*(11), 39–44.

Wachel, W. (1992). Managing the board and governing the organization. *Healthcare Executive, 7*(5), 29–31.

Waterman, R. A. (1994). Nonprofit medical care foundations. *Topics in Health Care Financing 20*(3), 13–18.

Whitman, P. A. (1994). Tax-exempt medical clinics. *Group Practice Journal, 43*(1), 42–44.

Wong, L. K. Specialty services capitation contracting for HMOs. *Medical Group Management Journal, 41*(5), 96–100.

Yarington, C. T. (1994). Tailor your group practice for the future. *Medical Group Management Update, 33*(1), 13.

Zinober, J. W. (1991). A physician's guide to practice governance. *Medical Group Management Journal, 38*(2), 54–56.